Necessity and Freedom

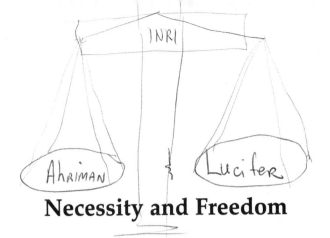

Necessity and Freedom

Rudolf Steiner

Five Lectures given in Berlin
between January 25 and February 8, 1916

Translated by Pauline Wehrle

Anthroposophic Press
Hudson, New York

Rudolf Steiner Press
London

The five lectures in this book are published in German under the title *Notwendigkeit und Freiheit im Weltengeschehen und im menschlichen Handeln* (Vol. 166 in the Bibliographic Survey).

Published in the United States of America by Anthroposophic Press, Bell's Pond, Star Route, Hudson, N. Y. 12534.

Published in the United Kingdom by Rudolf Steiner Press, 38 Museum Street, London, WC1.

Library of Congress Cataloging-in-Publication Data

Steiner, Rudolf, 1861-1925.
    [Notwendigkeit und Freiheit im Weltengeschehen und im menschlichen Handeln. English]
    Necessity and freedom : five lectures given in Berlin between January 25 and February 8, 1916 / Rudolf Steiner ; translated by Pauline Wehrle.
    Translation of: Notwendigkeit und Freiheit im Weltengeschehen und im menschlichen Handeln.
    1. Anthroposophy. 2. Free will and determinism. I. Title.
BP595.S894N6713   1988
123—dc19   88-9676
                                                                CIP

ISBN 0-88010-259-4 cloth Anthroposophic Press
        0-88010-260-8 pbk.
        85440-315-9 cloth Rudolf Steiner Press
        85440-325-6 pbk.

Cover: Graphic form by Rudolf Steiner, 1921
        Title lettering by Peter Stebbing

Printed in the United States of America

CONTENTS

The past shows us a picture of necessity. The future leaves the possibility open for freedom. Kant's antinomian chart. Limitation of logic when we approach infinity. An example with numbers. The Prague clock. Every external event has an elemental one underlying it. What is true on the physical plane often looks different on the spiritual plane. Beings are active on the elemental plane. In the physical realm things can be proved, whereas in the supersensible realm they are perceived. Mystery of Golgotha a free deed. Haeckel and the war.

The legend of the Prague clock and the workings of Ahriman and Lucifer. Law of cause and effect applies in the physical world. Historical events must be judged according to their intrinsic value. A condemnation of Goethe's *Faust*. Freedom and necessity mingle in human actions. Nature once a free deed of the gods. Past thoughts of the gods appear to us as necessity. Our present life of thought will be the outer nature of the future.

Illustration of three teachers with different attitudes to life, one is ahrimanic, another luciferic, and the third takes the path of progressive development. We must get to know the hidden forces behind ongoing events. Our actions can be influenced by pre-birth experiences. Two things combine in human beings, the stream of heredity and the spiritual part. Learning from life strengthens us.

Conflict of the Roman world and Teutonic tribes as basis of further historical development. Incursion of spiritual impulses in historical events. Unsuccessful actions are also necessary. Punishment as an enhancement of consciousness. *Faust* as an evolutionary factor. Greatest freedom involved in performing what is a necessity in world history. Empty space in world processes for certain impulses. Essential part of the will of angels is the intention. The animal in us as the cause of crime. Spiritual science now necessary, yet we can take it up in freedom. Right intentions lead to right results.

The *I* is found on the physical plane in acts of will. In the Middle Ages people still experienced auras. In the future the world will look bleaker and the will will have less strength. Spiritual science will bring consciousness of the aura and a strengthening of will. Human beings in the grip of dreaming and ecstasy. Necessity of developing thinking and willing. The true *I* found through the Christ impulse. We shall then have memory of past lives.

During the war years Rudolf Steiner spoke the following commemorative words before every lecture he gave to the Anthroposophical Society of countries affected by the war:

My dear friends, let us think of the guardian spirits of all the people out on the battlefields:

> Spirits ever watchful, guardians of your souls,
> May your pinions carry
> Our souls' imploring love
> To the human beings upon earth commited to your care;
> That, united with your power,
> Our prayer may radiate with help
> To the souls whom our love is seeking.

And let us turn to the guardian spirits of all those souls who have already passed through the portal of death because of the catastrophes of our time:

> Spirits ever watchful, guardians of your souls,
> May your pinions carry
> Our souls' imploring love
> To the human beings in the spheres committed to your care
> That, united with your power,
> Our prayer may radiate with help
> To the souls whom our love is seeking.

And may the Spirit whom we have for many years sought to approach with our spiritual science, the Spirit who passed through the Mystery of Golgotha for the salvation of the earth and the freedom and progress of humanity, may that spirit be with you in your arduous tasks.

Lecture I

Berlin, January 25, 1916

Now that we can be together again, it will be my task in the coming days to speak about important but rather difficult aspects of human and world existence, and we shall certainly not be able to reach any conclusion about these in *this* lecture; we can only make a beginning. As we proceed we will see how tremendously important these very questions are if we are to connect ourselves inwardly with the soul-stirring events of our times. If I had to summarize in a few words what I am going to speak about, I would say "necessity in world events and in human actions" and "human freedom in these two domains."

There is hardly anyone who is not more or less intensely concerned with these problems, and perhaps there are hardly any events on the physical plane that urge us as strongly to deal with these questions as the ones that are at present overshadowing the peoples of Europe and reverberating in their souls. If we look at world events and our own actions, feeling, willing, and thinking within these events, considering them for the moment in conjunction with what we call divine cosmic guidance, wisdom-filled cosmic guidance, we see that this divine guidance is at work everywhere. And if we look at something that has happened and that perhaps we ourselves have been involved in, we can ask afterwards "Was the reason for this event we were involved in so much a part of wise cosmic guidance that we can say it was inevitable for it to happen as it did, and we

1

ourselves could not have acted differently in it?" Or, looking more toward the future, we could also say "At some time in the future one or another thing will happen in which we believe we may be playing a part. Ought we not assume of the wise world guidance we presupposed that what happens in the future will also come about inevitably or, as we often say, is predetermined?" Can our freedom exist under such conditions? Can we resolve to use the ideas and skills we have acquired to intervene in some way? Can we do anything to alter things through the way we intervene if we do not want them to happen in the way they would be bound to happen without our intervention?

If we look back on the past, we tend to have the impression that everything was inevitable and could not have happened differently. If we look more toward the future, we have the impression that it must be possible for us to intervene in the course of events with our own will as much as we can. In short, we will always be in a conflict between supposing an absolute and all-pervading necessity on the one hand and necessarily assuming that we are free on the other. For without this latter assumption we cannot maintain our world view and would have to accept the fact that we are like cogs in the huge machine of existence, governed by the forces ruling the machine to the point where even the duties of the cogs are predetermined.

As you know, the conflict between choosing one thing or the other runs to some extent through all our intellectual endeavors. There have always been philosophers called determinists who supposed that all the events we are involved in through our actions and our willing are strictly predetermined, and there have also always been indeterminists who supposed that, on the contrary, human beings can intervene in the course of evolution through their will and their ideas. You know too that the most extreme form of determinism is fatalism, which clings so firmly to the belief that the world is pervaded by spiritual necessity as to presuppose that not one single thing could possibly happen differently from the way it was predetermined, that human beings cannot do other than submit passively to a fate that fills the whole world just because everything is predetermined.

Perhaps some of you also know that Kant set up an antinomian chart on one side of which he wrote a particular statement and always set its opposite on the other side.[1] For example, on one side stood the assertion "In terms of space the world is infinite," and on the other side "In terms of space the world is finite." He then went on to show that with the concepts at our disposal we can prove one of these just as well as the other. We can prove with the same logical exactitude that "the world is infinite with regard to both space and time" or that "the world is finite, boarded-up, in terms of space and that it had a beginning in time."

The questions we have introduced also belong among the ones Kant put on his antinomian chart. He drew people's attention to the fact that one can just as well prove positively, in as proper and logical a way as possible, that everything that happens in the world, including human action, is subject to rigid necessity, as one can prove that human beings are free and influence in one way or another the course of events when they bring their will to bear on it. Kant considered these questions to be outside the realm of human knowledge, to be questions that lie beyond the limits of human knowledge, because we can prove the one just as easily and conclusively as the other.

Our studies of the last few years will actually have

3

more or less given you the groundwork to get to the bottom of this strange mystery. For it certainly is a mysterious question whether human beings are bound by necessity or are free. It *is* a puzzling matter. Yet it is even more puzzling that both these alternatives can be conclusively proved. You will find no basis at all for overcoming doubt in this sphere if you look outside of what we call spiritual science. Only the background spiritual science can give will enable you to discover something about what is at the bottom of this mysterious question.

This time we will deal with our subject in very slow stages. I would just like to ask in anticipation, "How is such a thing possible that human beings can prove something and also prove its opposite?" When we approach a matter of this kind, we are certainly made aware of certain limits in normal human comprehension, in ordinary human logic. We meet with this limitation of human logic in regard to other things too. It always appears when human beings want to approach infinity with their concepts.

I can show you this by means of a very simple example. As soon as human beings want to approach infinity with their intellects, something occurs that can be called confusion in their concepts. I will demonstrate this in a very simple way. You must just be a little patient and follow a train of thought to which you are probably not accustomed. Suppose I write these figures on the blackboard one after the other, 1, 2, 3, 4, 5, and so on. I could write an infinite number of them: 1, 2, 3, 4, 5, 6, etc., couldn't I? I can also write a second column of figures; on the right of each number I can put double the number, like this:

1	2
2	4
3	6
4	8
5	10
6	12

and so on.

Again I can write an infinite number of them. Now you will agree with me that each number in the right-hand column is in the left-hand column too. I can underline 2, 4, 6, 8, and so on. Look at the left column for a moment; an infinite series of numbers is possible. This infinite series contains all the numbers included in the right column. 2, 4, 6, and so on are all there. I can continue underlining them. If you look at the figures that are underlined, you will see that they are exactly half of all the numbers together because every other one is underlined. But when I write them on the right-hand side, I can write 2, 4, 6, 8, and so on into infinity. I have an infinite number both on the left and on the right, and you cannot say that there are fewer on the right than on the left. There is no doubt that I am bound to have just as many numbers on the right as on the left.

And yet, as every other number would have to be crossed out on the left to make the left column the same as the right, the infinite number on the left is only half the infinite number on the right. Obviously I have just as many numbers on the right as on the left, namely an

$$5 \therefore \frac{\infty}{2} = \infty$$

infinite number, for each number on the right has one corresponding to it on the left—yet the amount of numbers on the right cannot but be half that of the numbers on the left.

There is no question about it, as soon as we deal with infinity, our thinking becomes confused. The problem arising here also cannot be solved, for it is just as true that on the right there are half as many numbers as on the left as it is true that there are exactly as many numbers on the right as on the left. Here you have the problem in its simplest form.

This brings us to the realization that our concepts cannot actually be used where infinity is concerned, where we go beyond the sense world—and infinity does go beyond the sense world. And do not imagine this to apply only to unlimited infinity, for you cannot use your concepts where limited infinity is concerned either, as the same confusion arises there.

Suppose you draw a triangle, a square, a pentagon, a hexagon and so on. When you reach a construction with a hundred sides, you will have come very close to a circle. You will no longer be able to distinguish the small lines very clearly, especially if you look at them from a distance. Therefore you can say that a circle is a polygon with an infinite number of sides. If you have a small circle there are an infinite number of sides in it; if you have a circle twice the size, you still have an infinite number of sides—and yet exactly twice as many!

So you do not need to go as far as unlimited infinity, for if you take a small circle with an infinite number of sides and a circle twice the size with an infinite number of sides, then even in the realm of visible, limited infinity you can encounter something that throws your concepts into utter confusion. What I have just said is extremely important. For people completely fail to notice that there is only a certain field where our concepts apply, namely the field of the physical plane, and that there is a particular reason why this has to be so.

You know, at a place where people are attacking us rather severely—which is now happening in many places from a great many people—a pastor gave a speech opposing our spiritual science, and thinking it might be especially effective, he concluded with a quotation from Matthias Claudius.[2] This quotation says roughly that human beings are really poor sinners who cannot know much and ought to rest content with what they do know and not chase after what they cannot know. The pastor picked this verse out of a poem by Matthias Claudius because he thought he could charge us with wanting to transcend the sense world—after all, had not Matthias Claudius already said that human beings are nothing but sinners who are unable to get beyond this world of the senses?

"By chance," as people say, a friend of ours looked up this poem by Matthias Claudius and also read the verse preceding it. This preceding verse says that a person can go out into the open and, although the moon is always a round orb, if it does not happen to be full moon, he sees only part of the moon even though the other part is there. In the same way there are many things in the world people could become aware of if only they looked at them at the right moment. Thus Matthias Claudius wanted to draw attention to the fact that people should not confine themselves to immediate sense appearance and that anyone who allows himself to be deceived by this is a poor sinner. In fact, what the good pastor quoted from Matthias Claudius reflected on himself.

The sense world—if we happen not to be just like that pastor—at times makes us aware that wherever we look we should also look in the opposite direction and adjust our first view accordingly. However, the world of the senses cannot supply this immediate adjustment with regard to what transcends the sense world. We cannot just quote the other verse. That is why human beings philosophize away and, of course, are convinced of the truth of their speculations, for they can be logically proved. But their opposite can also be logically proved. So let us tackle the question today, "Why is it that when we transcend the sense world our thinking gets so confused?" And we will now look at the question in a way which will bring us closer to an answer. How does it happen that two contradictory statements can both be proved right? We will find this has to do with the fact that human life is in a kind of central position, a point of balance between two polar opposite forces, the ahrimanic and the luciferic.

You can of course cogitate on freedom and necessity and imagine you have compelling evidence that the world contains only necessity. But the compelling force of this argument comes from Ahriman. When we prove things in one direction, it is Ahriman who leads us astray, and if we prove their opposite, we are misled by Lucifer. For we are always exposed to these two powers, and if we do not take into account that we are placed in between them, we shall never get to the bottom of the conflicts in human nature, such as the one we have been considering.

It was actually in the course of the nineteenth century that people lost the feeling that throughout the world order there are, besides a state of equilibrium, pendulum swings to the right and the left, a swing toward Ahriman and a swing toward Lucifer. This feeling has been totally lost. After all, if you speak nowadays of Ahriman and Lucifer, you are considered not quite

8

sane, aren't you? It was not as bad as this until the middle of the nineteenth century, for a very clever philosopher, Thrandorff, wrote a very nice article here in Berlin in the middle of the nineteenth century in an attempt to refute the argument of a certain clergyman.[3] This clergyman let it be known—and it should be alright to say this in our circles—that there is no devil and that it is really a dreadful superstition to speak of one. We speak of Ahriman rather than of the devil. The philosopher Thrandorff spoke out against the clergyman in a very interesting article, "The Devil: No Dogmatic Bogy." As late as the middle of the 1850s he tried as it were to prove the existence of Ahriman on a strictly philosophical basis.

In the course of the public lectures I am to give here in the near future I hope I can speak about this extinct part of human spiritual life, about an aspect of theosophy that completely disappeared in the middle of the nineteenth century. Right up to that time people had still spoken about these things, even if they called them by other names. The feeling for these things has now been lost, but basically it was there in a delicate form right into the fourteenth and fifteenth centuries, until it had to recede into the background for a while in the natural course of things. We know of course, as I have often emphasized, that spiritual science does not in the slightest way deny the great value and significance of progress in the natural sciences. But this progress in science would not have been possible unless the feeling for this opposition between Ahriman and Lucifer, which can be discovered only on a spiritual level, had been lost. It now has to emerge again above the threshold of human consciousness.

I would like to give you an example of how things stood in regard to Ahriman and Lucifer in the days when people had only a feeling left that there are two different powers at work. Here is an example to illustrate this.

In the old town hall in Prague there is a remarkable clock that was made in the fifteenth century. This clock is really a marvel. At first sight it looks like a sort of sundial, but it is so intricately constructed that it shows the course of the hours in a twofold way: the old Bohemian and the modern way. In the old Bohemian way the hours went from 1 or rather from 0 to 24, and the other way only to 12. At sunset the pointer or gnomon—and there was a shadow there—always pointed to 1. The clock was so arranged that the pointer literally always indicated 1 at sunset. That is to say, despite the varying times of sunset the hand always showed 1.

In addition to this, the clock also showed when sun or moon eclipses occurred. It also showed the course of the various planets through the constellations, giving the planetary orbits. It really was a wonderful construction and even showed the movable festivals, that is to say, it indicated on what day Easter fell in a particular year. It was also a calendar, giving the course of the year from January to December, including the fact that Easter is movable. A special pointer showed on what day Easter fell, despite it being movable, and it also showed Whitsun.

This clock, then, was constructed in the fifteenth century in an extraordinarily impressive way. And the story of how it was constructed has been investigated. But apart from this story—and the documents are there for you to read, with lots of descriptions—there is a legend that also aims at giving an account of the marvellous quality of this clock: first regarding its wonderful construction, and then regarding the fact that the man who was gifted enough to make such a clock always wound it up as long as he lived. After his death nobody could wind it, and they searched everywhere for people who could put it in order and get it going. As a rule they only found people who damaged it. Then someone would be found who said he could sort it out and did so, yet time and again the clock went wrong.

These facts grew into a kind of folk tale, which runs as follows: Once upon a time through a special gift from heaven a simple man acquired the ability to make this clock. He alone knew how to look after it. The legend attaches great significance to the fact that he was only a simple man who acquired this ability through special grace; that is to say, he was inspired by the spiritual world. But it came about that the governor wanted to keep this clock specially for Prague and prevent any other town from having one like it. So he had the inspired clockmaker blinded by having his eyes plucked out. Thus the man withdrew from the scene. But just before his death he begged once more to be permitted a moment in which to set the clock to rights again, and according to the legend he used this moment to make a quick manipulation and put the clock into such disorder that nobody could ever put it right again.

At first sight this seems a very unpretentious story. But in the way the story is constructed there is a sure feeling for the existence of Ahriman and Lucifer and the balance between them. Think how sensitively this story has been formed. The same sensitive construction can be found in countless such folk tales; it grows out of this same sure feeling for Lucifer and Ahriman. The story begins with the position of equilibrium, doesn't it? Through an act of grace from the spiritual world the man acquires the ability to construct an extraordinary clock. There is no trace of egotism in it, though anybody can give way to egotism. It was a gift of grace, and he really did not build the clock out of egotism. Nor was there any intellectuality in it, for it is expressly stated that he was a simple man. This whole description of the skill being an act of grace with no trace of egotism, and of his being a simple man who was free of intellectuality, was in fact given in order to indicate that there was no trace of Ahriman and Lucifer in this man's soul, but that he was entirely under the influence of divine powers that were good and progressive.

Lucifer lived in the governor. It was out of egotism that he wanted to keep the clock exclusively for his own town, and this was why he blinded the clockmaker. Lucifer is placed on the one side. But as soon as Lucifer is there, he always allies himself with his brother Ahriman. And because the man has been blinded, this other power acquires the capacity to attack from outside through skillful manipulation. That is the work of Ahriman.

Thus the power for good is placed between Lucifer and Ahriman. You can find a sensitive construction like this in many of the folk tales, even the simplest of them. But it was possible for this feeling of the intervention of Ahriman and Lucifer in life to get lost at a time when a sense had to gain ground that positive and negative electricity, positive and negative magnetism, and so on, are the basic forces of the material world. This feeling for perceiving the world spiritually had to withdraw in order for scientific investigation to flourish.

We shall now look at how Ahriman and Lucifer intervene in what human beings call knowledge, in what people call their relation to the world in general, in a way that leads to the very confusion we were speaking about. This confusion is especially evident in the questions we have introduced. Let us take a simple hypothetical example. I could just as well have taken this from great world events as from everyday occurrences. Let us suppose that three or four people are preparing to go out for a drive. They plan to travel, let us say, through a mountain pass. This pass has overhanging rocks. The people are ready for the drive and intend setting out at an arranged time. But the chauffeur has just ordered another mug of beer which is served a bit too late. He therefore delays the departure by five minutes. Then he sets out with the party. They drive through the ravine. Just as they come to the overhanging rock it breaks loose, falls on top of the vehicle, and crushes the whole party. They all perish, or perhaps it was only the passengers who were killed and the chauffeur was spared.

5 min. Delay [handwritten margin note]

Here we have a case in point. You could ask whether it was the chauffeur's fault, or whether the whole thing was governed by absolute necessity. Was it absolutely inevitable that these people should meet with this disaster at that precise moment? And was the chauffeur's tardiness just part of this necessity? Or could we imagine that if only the chauffeur had been punctual, he would have driven them through the mountain pass a long time before the rock fell, and they would never have been hit by it?

Here in the midst of everyday life you have this question of freedom and necessity which is intimately connected with "guilty" or "innocent." Obviously, if everything is subject to absolute necessity, we cannot say that the chauffeur was guilty at all from a higher point of view, as it was entirely inevitable that these people met their death.

We meet this problem in life all the time. It is, as we have said, one of the most difficult of questions, the kind of question in which Ahriman and Lucifer interfere most easily when we try to find a solution. Ahriman is the one who appears first when this question is being tackled, as we shall see.

We will have to approach this question from a different angle if we want to get at an answer. You see, if we set about solving a question like this by starting with the thought "I can easily follow the course of events: the boulder fell—that happened," and then ask "Is this actually based on necessity or freedom? Could things have happened differently?" we are only looking at the external events. We are looking at the events as they happen on the physical plane. Now people follow this approach out of the same impulse that leads them, if they have a materialistic outlook, to stop short at the physical body when contemplating the human being. Anyone who knows nothing about spiritual science *will* stop short at the physical body nowadays, won't he? He will say "The human being you see and feel is what exists." He does not go beyond the physical body to the etheric body. And if he is a thoroughly pig-headed materialist, he will jeer and scoff when he hears people saying there is a finer, etheric body underlying the dense physical body. Yet you know how well-founded the view is that among the members of the human being the etheric body is the one most closely associated with the physical body, and in the course of time we have become accustomed to knowing that we must not just speak of the human physical body but also of the human etheric body, and so on.

Some of you, however, may not yet have asked yourselves "What kind of world is that other world outside the human being, the world in which the ordinary world events occur?" We have of course spoken of a number of things in this connection. We have said that to begin with when we perceive the external events of the physical plane with our senses, we have no idea that wherever we look there are elemental beings; it is exactly the same when we first look at the human being.

Human beings have an etheric body, which we have often also called an elemental body. Outside in nature, in external physical happenings in general, we have a succession of physical events and also the world of elemental existence. This runs absolutely parallel: the human being with a physical and an etheric body, and physical processes with events of the elemental world flowing into them. It would be just as one-sided to say that external processes are merely physical as to say that a human being has a physical body only, when we ought to be saying that he also has an etheric body. What we perceive with our physical senses and physical intellect is one thing. But there is something behind it that is analogous to the human etheric body. Behind every external physical occurrence there is a higher, more subtle one.

There are people who have a certain awareness of such things. This awareness can come to them in two different ways. You may have noticed something like the following either in yourself or in other people. A person has had some experience. But afterwards he comes to you and says—or it may be something you experienced and you may say, "Actually I had the feeling that while this experience was taking place externally, something quite different was happening to me as well, in a higher part of my being." This is to say, deeper natures may feel that events not taking place on the physical plane at all can yet have an important effect on the course of their life. First, such people know something has happened to them. Others go even further and see things of this kind symbolically in a dream. Someone dreams he experiences this or that. He dreams, for instance, that he is killed by a boulder. He wakes up and is able to say, "That was a symbolic dream; something has taken place in my soul life." It can often be proved true in life that something took place in the soul that was of far greater significance than what happened to the person on the physical plane. He may have progressed a stage higher in knowledge, purified part of his will nature, or made his feelings more sensitive or something of that kind.

In lectures given here recently I drew attention to the fact that what a person knows with his *I* is actually only a part of all that happens to him, and that the astral body knows a very great deal more, though not consciously. You will remember my telling you this. The astral body certainly knows of a great deal that happens to us in the supersensible realm and not in the realm of the senses. Now we have arrived from another direction at the fact that something is continually happening to us in the supersensible realm. Just as in the case of my moving my hand, the physical movement is only part of the whole process and behind it there is an etheric process, a process of my etheric body, so every physical process outside me is permeated by a subtle elementary process that runs parallel with it and takes place in the supersensible realm. Not only beings are permeated by a supersensible element, but so is the whole of existence.

Remember something I have repeatedly referred to and which even seems somewhat paradoxical. I have pointed out that in the spiritual realm we often have the opposite of what exists on the physical plane, not always, but often. Thus if something is true here for the physical plane, the truth with regard to the spiritual aspect can look quite different. Not always, as I say. But I have counted many cases over the years where one would have to say that on the spiritual level there is exactly the opposite result from what one would expect to happen on the physical plane.

With regard to supersensible occurrences running parallel with those of the sense world, this is occasionally, in fact very often, the case. So let us examine it. If we see a party of people setting off by coach and taking a drive, and a piece of rock falls and crushes them, that is the physical occurrence. Parallel with this physical event, that is to say, within it in the same way as our etheric body is within us, there is a supersensible occurrence. And we have to recognize that this may be the exact opposite of what is happening here on the physical plane. In fact it is very frequently the exact opposite.

This can also create great confusion if we do not watch out. For instance, the following may happen. If someone has acquired atavistic clairvoyance and has a kind of second sight, he or she may have the following experience: Supposing a party of people is setting out on a journey, but at the last moment one of the party decides to stay behind, the person who has second sight, let us say. Instead of going with the others, that person stays behind and after a while has a vision. In this vision any event can appear to that person. He or she could of course just as well see the party being hit by boulders as see, for instance—and this can be a matter of disposition—that some especially good fortune happens to them. He or she could very well see the party having a very joyful experience, and might subsequently hear that the party had perished in the way I described.

This could happen if the clairvoyant were not to see what was happening on the physical plane—which he might very well have seen—but had seen what was happening as a parallel event on the astral plane: for the moment these people left the physical plane they may well have been called to something special in the spiritual world, something that filled them with an abundance of new life in the spiritual world. In short, the clairvoyant person may have seen an event of the supersensible worlds going on in exactly the opposite direction, and this absolutely contradictory event could be true. It might really be the case that here on the physical plane a misfortune exists that corresponds in the supersensible world to some great good fortune for those same souls.

Now someone who thinks he is smarter than the wise guidance of the world (and there are such people) might say, "If I ruled the world, I would not do it in such a way that I call souls to happiness in the spiritual world and at the same time shower them with misfortune here on the physical plane. I would do it better than that!" Well, all one can say to people like that is, "Surely one can understand that here on the physical plane people can easily be misled by Ahriman. But cosmic wisdom always knows better." It could be a matter of the following: The task awaiting the souls in the spiritual world requires their having this experience here on the physical plane, so that they can look back, so to speak, to this physical event of their earthly lives and gain a certain strength they need. That is to say, for the souls who experience them these two occurrences, the physical and the spiritual one, may necessarily belong together.

We could quote hypothetical examples of all kinds, showing that when something takes place here on the physical plane there exists, as it were, an etheric body of this event, an elemental, supersensible event belonging to it. We must not merely generalize like pantheists do and stop short at the general statement that there is a spiritual world underlying the physical, but we must give concrete examples. We must be aware that behind

18

every physical occurrence there is a spiritual occurrence, a real spiritual occurrence, and both together form a whole.

If we follow the course of events on the physical plane, we can say that we get to the point where we link together the events of the physical plane by means of thoughts. And as we watch things happen on the physical plane we actually reach the point of finding a "cause" for each "effect." That is how things are. People everywhere look for the cause belonging to each effect. Whenever anything has happened, people always have to find the cause of it. But this means finding the inevitability. If you look with sufficient pedantry at the simple example I chose, you could say, "Well now, this party had gathered and had fixed their departure for a definite time. But if I follow up why the chauffeur was tardy, I will go in several directions. First of all, I may look at the chauffeur himself and consider how he was brought up and how he became tardy. Then I will look at the various circumstances leading to his getting his mug of beer too late. All I will be able to find in this way is merely a chain of causes. I will be able to show how one event fits in with the others in such a way that the affair could not possibly have happened otherwise. I will gradually come to the point where I completely eliminate the chauffeur's free will, for if we have a cause for every effect, this includes everything the chauffeur does as well." The chauffeur only wanted another mug of beer, didn't he, because he had probably not been thrashed sufficiently when he was young. If he had been thrashed more often—and it is not his fault that he was not—things would not have turned out as they did. Looking at it this way we can base the whole thing on a chain of cause and effect.

This has to do with the fact that it is only on the

physical plane that we can use concepts. For just consider: if you want to understand something, one thought must be able to follow from another, that is to say, you depend on being able to develop one thought out of another. It lies in the nature of concepts that one follows from the other. That must be so.

Yet, what can be clearly and necessarily linked together through concepts on the physical plane immediately changes as soon as we enter the neighboring supersensible world. There we have to do not with cause and effect but with beings. This is where beings are active. At every moment one or another being is working on or withdrawing from a task. There it is not at all a matter of what can be grasped by concepts in the usual sense.

If you tried using concepts for what is happening in the spiritual world, the following could happen. You might think, "Well, here I am. Certainly I am far enough advanced to perceive that something spiritual is happening. At one moment a gnome approaches, then a sylph, and soon afterwards another being. Now all the beings are together. I will do my best to fathom what the effects will have to be." On the physical plane this is sometimes easy to do, of course. If we hit a billiard ball in a certain direction, we know which way the other one will go, because we can calculate it. Yet on the spiritual plane it may happen that when you have seen a being and now know "Ah, that is a gnome, he is setting out to do something and will do such and such; he is joining forces with another being, thus the following is bound to happen," you think you have figured it all out. But the next moment another being appears and changes the whole thing, or a being you were counting on drops out and disappears and no longer participates. There, everything is based on beings. You cannot link everything together with your concepts in the same way as you can on the physical plane. That is quite impossible. There, you cannot explain one thing following from the other on the basis of concepts. Things work together in an entirely different manner in the spiritual world, in the series or stream of spiritual happenings running parallel with physical happenings.

We must become familiar with the fact that underlying our world there is a world we must not only assume to be spiritual in comparison to ours, but we must also assume its events to be connected with each other in a totally different way than those in our world. For we can do nothing at all in the spiritual world, in the actual reality of this spiritual world, with the way we are used to explaining things in the world of our concepts.

Thus we see that two worlds interpenetrate; one of them can be grasped with concepts and the other cannot, but can only be perceived. I am pointing to something that goes very deep, but people are not aware how deep it goes. Just consider for a moment that if someone were to believe he could prove everything, and that only what has been proved is true, the following could happen. That person could say, "As a matter of fact, everything has to be proved, and what has not been proved is unacceptable. Therefore everything that happens in the course of the history of the world must be capable of being proved. So I only need to think hard and I am bound to be able to prove, for instance, whether the Mystery of Golgotha took place or not." Indeed, people are so very inclined nowadays to say that if the Mystery of Golgotha cannot be proved, the whole thing is nonsense and there never was such an event.

And what do people think of proofs? They think that

21

one starts with one definite concept and proceeds from this to the next one, and if it is possible to do this right through, the matter is proved. But no world other than the physical functions according to this kind of proof. This reasoning does not apply to any other world. For if we were able to prove that the Mystery of Golgotha had to take place of necessity, and this could be concluded from our concepts, it would not have been a free deed at all! Christ would then have been *compelled* to come down to the earth from the cosmos simply because human concepts prove and therefore dictate it. However, the Mystery of Golgotha has to be a free deed, that is to say, it has to be just the kind of deed that cannot be proved. It is important that people come to realize this.

It is the same thing, after all, when people want to prove either that God created the world or that he did not. There, too, they proceed from one thought to another. But "creating the world," at any rate will have been a free deed of a divine being! From this it follows that we cannot prove the Creation as following of necessity from our series of concepts; rather, we have to perceive it to arrive at it.

So we are saying something of tremendous importance when we state that the very next world to ours—which, as a supersensible world, permeates ours—is not organized in a way we can penetrate by means of our concepts and their conclusiveness, but that there a kind of vision comes into its own in which events are arranged in a totally different way.

Today I would just like to add a few words about the following. When I was here at Christmas, I drew your attention to the fact that in our time especially, such contradictory things are emerging, that they are quite confusing for human thinking. Just imagine, a book has just been published by the great scientist Ernst Haeckel called *Thoughts about Eternity*.[4] I have already mentioned it earlier. These *Thoughts about Eternity* contain exactly the opposite of what many other people have concluded as a result of living through recent world events. Just think, there are many people today (we shall come to speak of this fact in its particular connection with our present studies, but today I just wanted to give an introduction) who have experienced a deepening of their religious feelings just because world events are having such a terribly overwhelming effect on their souls; for they say, "Unless there is a supersensible world underlying our physical world, how can we explain what is happening in our time?" Many people have rediscovered their feeling for religion. I do not need to describe their train of thought; it is obvious and can be discerned in so many people.

Haeckel arrives at a different train of thought. He explains in his recently published book that people believe in immortality of the soul. However, he says, current events prove clearly enough that any such belief is ridiculous, for we witness thousands of people perishing every day for no reason at all. With these events in mind, how can any sensible person imagine that there can be any talk about the immortality of the soul? How is it possible for a higher world order to stand behind things of this sort?

These shocking events seem to Haeckel to prove his dogma that one cannot speak of immortality of the soul. Here we have antinomy again: A large proportion of humanity is experiencing a deepening of religious feeling, while the very same events are making Haeckel tremendously superficial where religion is concerned.

All this is connected with the fact that nowadays people are unable to understand the relationship between the world accessible to their senses and their brain-bound intellect and the supersensible world underlying it. No sooner do they approach these things than their thinking gets confused. Yet despite all the disillusionment it brings, our time will certainly in one way also bring about a deepening of people's souls, a turning away from materialism. It will be necessary that knowledge of the way supersensible events complement happenings in the world of the senses arise from a pure activity of the soul devoting itself to an impartial exploration of the world. It is necessary that there should be at least a small number of people who are able to realize that all the pain and suffering being experienced at present on the physical plane are, from the point of view of the whole of human evolution, only one side and that there is also another side, a supersensible side.

We have drawn your attention to this supersensible aspect from various points of view, and we will speak of still further ones. But when peace returns to Europe's blood-stained soil, we will again and again experience the need for a group of people capable of hearing and sensing spiritually what the spiritual worlds will then be saying to humanity in times of peace. And we must never tire of impressing the following lines upon our hearts and souls, for it will be proved over and over again how deeply true they are:

> Out of the courage of the fighters,
> Out of the blood of battles,
> Out of the grief of the bereaved,
> Out of the peoples' deeds of sacrifice
> There shall arise spirit fruit
> If only souls, in spirit-mindfulness,
> Will reach out to the spirits' realm.

24

Lecture II

January 27, 1916

The day before yesterday I endeavored to show you the universal mystery of necessity and freedom in its two equally significant aspects: world processes and human action. I began by drawing your attention to the full significance and difficulty of this mystery that is both cosmic and human, and today we will continue along the same lines. I used a hypothetical example demonstrating this difficulty in regard to world events. I said, "Suppose a party of people had set out to drive through a ravine where there is an overhanging rock, and had arranged to go at a definite time. The chauffeur, however, is negligent and delays the departure by five minutes. Because of this, the party arrives at the spot beneath the rock at the very moment when the rock falls down." According to external judgment, and I say "external" deliberately, one would have to say that all those people were buried beneath the rock because of the chauffeur's negligence, that is, because of a circumstance that was apparently someone's fault.

Last time I wanted mainly to emphasize that we should not approach a problem of this sort too hastily with our ordinary thinking and believe we can solve it that way. I showed that in the first place we use our thinking only for the physical plane, therefore it has become accustomed to dealing with those requirements only, and gets confused if we go a bit beyond these.

I would like today to go on to show the serious nature of the whole problem. For we shall not be able to approach any kind of solution in the lecture intended for Sunday, unless we also examine all the implications for human knowledge itself, unless we fully examine why we get lost in blind alleys of thinking precisely in life's most difficult problems, why we are, so to speak, lost in the woods and imagining we are making progress when we are really just going round in circles. We do not notice we are going round in circles until we realize we are back at our starting point again. The strange thing is that where our thinking is concerned, we do not notice that we return again and again to the same point. We will have more to say about this.

I have indicated that this important problem has to do with what we call the ahrimanic and luciferic forces in world events and in what approaches the human being in his actions and his whole thinking, feeling, and willing. I mentioned that as late as the fifteenth century people had a feeling that just as positive and negative electricity play a part in natural processes, and no physicist would hesitate to speak about them, so Ahriman and Lucifer could also be seen in events of the world, even if people did not use these names. I showed this by the apparently remote example of the clock in the old town hall of Prague that is so ingeniously constructed that in addition to being a clock it is also a sort of calendar showing the course of the planets and eclipses of the sun and moon. In fact, it is a great work of art created by a very talented man. I told you that there are documents showing that it was a professor of a Prague university who made this work of art, though this point is of no further interest to us, for those are only the processes that took place on the physical plane.

I explained that a simple folk tale grew out of the feeling that in an affair of this sort ahrimanic and luciferic forces play their part. The story tells us that this

26

clock in the Prague town hall was made beautifully by a simple man who received the power to create it entirely through a kind of divine inspiration. The story then goes on to say that the governor wanted to keep this clock all for himself and would not allow anything like it to be made in any other town. So he had the clockmaker blinded and forced him to retire. Not until he felt death approaching was the clockmaker allowed to touch the clock again. And then, with skillful manipulation, he gave the clock such a jolt that it could actually never be put right again.

In this folk tale we feel that on the one hand there was a sensing of the luciferic principle in the governor who wanted to have sole possession of the clock that could only be constructed by a gift of grace from the good, progressive powers, and that as soon as Lucifer appeared, he was joined by Ahriman, for the clockmaker's ruining of the clock was an ahrimanic deed. The moment Lucifer is summoned—and the opposite is also the case—he is countered by Ahriman. It is not only in the composition of this story that we see people's feeling for Ahriman and Lucifer, we also see it in another aspect, namely in the form of the clock itself. We see that the clockmaker, too, wanted to include ahrimanic and luciferic forces in the very construction of the clock, for besides all that I have already told you of its artistic perfection, this clock included something else as well. Apart from the clock face, the planetary dial, and all the other things it had, there were figures on both sides of the clock, Death on one side and two figures on the other. One of these figures was a man holding a money-bag containing money he could jingle, and the other figure represented a man holding a mirror in which he could see himself all the time.

These two figures are exceptionally good examples

of the person who gives himself up to external values: the rich miser, the ahrimanic person—and the luciferic person who wants perpetually to have his vanity aroused, the man looking at himself in the mirror. The clockmaker himself confronts ahrimanic and luciferic qualities and on the other side there is Death, the balancer (we shall say more about this later), put there as a reminder that through the constant alternation of life between death and birth and between birth and death human beings rise above the sphere in which Ahriman and Lucifer are active. Thus in the clock itself we see a wonderful presentation of the feeling still existing at that time for the ahrimanic and luciferic element.

We must bring a feeling for this element to life again in a certain way if we want to solve the difficult question we have introduced. Basically the world always confronts us as a duality. Look at nature. Mere nature always bears the stamp of rigid necessity. In fact, we know that it is the scientists' ideal to be able to calculate future occurrences mathematically on the basis of past ones. Ideally, scientists would like to deal with all natural phenomena in the same way as with future sun and moon eclipses, which can be predicted through calculations based on the constellations in the heavens. In relation to natural phenomena people feel they are confronting absolute rigid necessity. Ever since the fifteenth century people have grown accustomed to accepting rigid necessity as the model for their world outlook. This has gradually led to historical phenomena also being perceived as imbued with a similar rigid necessity.

Yet where historical phenomena are concerned we should also consider another aspect. Let us take an example quite apart from our own life situation, for instance, Goethe as a historical phenomenon.[1] In certain respects we also are inclined to regard the appearance of Goethe and all he produced as being based on a sort of rigid necessity. But someone might bring the argument "Goethe was born on August 28, 1749. If this boy had not been born into this family, what would have happened? Would we have had Goethe's works?" It might be pointed out that Goethe himself refers to the fact that his father and mother brought him up in a special way, each contributing something toward what he later became. Would his works have been created if he had been brought up differently? Again, let us look at Goethe's meeting with Karl August, Duke of Weimar.[2] If the duke had not called Goethe to him and given him the kind of life we know he had from the 1770s onward, would entirely different works have resulted? Or might not Goethe even have been quite an ordinary cabinet secretary if he had been brought up differently at home, and the poetic urge had not already been so alive in him? What would German literature and art after Goethe's time have been like if all these things had been different?

All these questions can be asked, and they show the very profound significance of this question. But we have not yet fully arrived at an answer which would be other than superficial. We can go deeper still and ask different questions. Let us return to the artist who made the old Prague town hall clock. He put on it the figures of the rich miser with the money-bag, the vain man and, opposite them, Death. Now it is possible to say that the man accomplished something by putting the figures there. But if we express it like that, we are naming a cause of countless possible effects. For just imagine how many people have stood in front of that rich miser, the vain man looking at his reflection, and Death. And how many people have also seen an even smarter thing the clockmaker arranged. Namely, every time the clock was about to strike, Death began to move first, accompanying the striking of the hour with a ringing apparatus, then the other figure moved. Death nodded to the miser and the latter nodded back. All these things were there to be seen, and they were important guides for life. They made a deep impression on the beholder.

We see this from the fact that the folk tale goes on to relate something unusual. Whenever the clock was about to strike, the skeleton, Death, opened its mouth and people saw inside it a sparrow that longed for nothing more than to break free. But just as it was about to do so, the mouth closed, and it was shut in again for an hour. People told an ingenious legend about this opening and shutting of the mouth, showing what a significant thing "time" is—what we so abstractly call "time" and "the marching on of time." They wanted to give an indication that there are deep secrets hidden here.

Let us imagine that a person might have stood in front of the clock. I want to mention this folk tale as an indication of the thoughts a person might have about it, or rather the imaginations a person might see, for that sparrow was not mere invention. Some of the people who looked at the clock saw the sparrow as an imagination. I just wanted to mention that. Let us look at it rationally for a moment. A person in a state of moral uncertainty might observe the clock and see Death nodding both to the rich man, who has become dependent on his riches, and to the vain man. And the impression this has on him could divert him from the possibility of being misled in his own state of moral wavering.

We can also imagine something else. Taking this aspect into consideration we could say that the man who constructed this work of art through divine inspiration has done a great deal of good. For a lot of people may have looked at this work of art and improved morally in certain respects. It might be said what a favorable karma this man must have had, being able to have a good effect on so many people's souls! And one might begin to wonder just how many people's souls he had helped by means of this imagination. One might begin to think of the artist's karma. One might say that the making of that clock and placing Death and Ahriman and Lucifer upon it was the most wonderful starting point for a favorable karma. One might indulge in such an outlook and say that there are people who trigger off a whole series of good deeds by means of one single deed. So this series of good deeds must be put down in their karma. And one could begin to wonder how each of one's own deeds should be carried out so that a similar series of good deeds can arise.

Here you see the beginning of a train of thought that can go astray. An attempt to think out how to set about doing deeds that produce a series of good deeds would be nonsense when it comes to making it a principle of life, wouldn't it? Someone might suggest that a stream of good deeds does spring from what that man did. But someone else could argue "No, I have followed up the matter of this clock and am convinced that there has not been much in the way of such results." That person might be a pessimist and say that times are too evil for such good effects. People do not believe it when they see things like that. He has seen something quite different happening in many cases. He has seen people looking at the clock who had a democratic frame of mind and a smoldering hatred of the rich. And when a person like that saw the clock, he noticed that it was only the rich man to whom Death nodded and who nodded back. "I will put that into practice" he said, looked for

PAY IT FORWARD

the first miser he could find and murdered him. Similar deeds of hatred were done by other people. The clockmaker brought all these about through his work of art. That is what will have to be put down in his karma.

And again, taking a shortsighted view, someone could say "Perhaps after all one should not make a perfect work of art, one that has great inner value, because it might have the worst possible effects; it might have countless bad effects on one's karma."

This draws our attention to an immense temptation for the whole range of human soul capacities and knowledge. For one only needs to look at oneself a little to see that people have the greatest inclination to ask about everything, "What was the result of it?" and to estimate the value of what has been done in accordance with the results. But in the same way as we started to speculate when we tried to think out whether the double numbers in the right column were as many as those in the left column or half as many, which was the example I gave you last time—just as we became mentally confused then, we are bound to become confused in our thinking now if we want to judge our actions by asking, "What result will they have, what effect will they have on my karma?"

Here again the folk tale is wiser, even more scientific, in the sense of spiritual science. For it is a very trivial thing to say, of course, but the folk tale does say that the clockmaker was a simple man. He had no intentions beside the thought that inspired him; he made the clock according to that, and did not speculate on what the results of his deed might be in any direction.

True, it cannot be denied—and this is what is so tempting—that you really may get somewhere if you think along these lines and ask what the results of a deed will be. It is tempting for the very reason that there are such things as actions where you have to ask what the consequences will be. And it would obviously be one-sided to draw the conclusion from what I have said that we should always behave like that clockmaker and not consider the consequences of our actions. For you have to have the consequences in mind if you thrash a boy for having been lazy. There are obviously cases like this where we have to have the consequences in mind. However, here lies the very point we must take to heart and examine closely, namely, that we relate to the world in two ways.

On the one hand, we receive impressions from the physical plane, and on the other hand we receive impressions from the spiritual world, as indicated in the legend, when it tells us that the artist was a simple man inspired by a gift of grace from above. When we are given these impressions by the spiritual world, when our souls are stimulated to do a particular thing, those are the moments in life when we have a second kind of certainty, a second kind of truth—not in an objective but a subjective sense—when we are guided by truth, we have a second kind of certainty, which is direct, and which we cannot but accept as such. This is the root of the matter.

On the one hand we are in the physical world, and in this world it looks as though every event follows naturally from the preceding one. But we are also within the spiritual world. In the last lecture I tried to show that just as we have an etheric body within our physical body, there is also a supersensible element active in the whole stream of events of the physical world. We are also placed within this supersensible activity, and from this proceed those impulses that are absolutely unique and that we have to follow quite regardless of the results, especially those in the physical world. Because human beings are in the world, they acquire a kind of certainty when they examine external things. This is how people observe nature. Observing natural phenomena is the only way to come to any certainty about cause and effect. On the other hand, however, we can receive direct certainty if we want it, by really opening our souls to its influences. Then we have to stop and give our full attention to a phenomenon, and know to evaluate it on the basis of its intrinsic value.

This, of course, is difficult. Yet we are constantly being given a chance, a crucial one, by the very phenomena themselves, particularly historical ones, to appreciate events and processes according to their intrinsic value. This is always necessary. But if we go more closely into questions that would lead us very far if we understood them rightly, we find a sphere where confusion in thinking is very marked. As a rule this confusion cannot be controlled by the individual. Let us take the phenomenon of Goethe's *Faust*.[3] It is an artistic creation, isn't it? There will be very few people in this hall, particularly as we have made a number of studies of *Faust*, who will not hold the opinion that Goethe's *Faust* is a great work of art, one that is tantamount to an inspiration of grace.

Through Goethe's *Faust*, German cultural life in a sense conquered the cultural life of other nations too. Even in Goethe's lifetime *Faust* had a strong influence on many people. They regarded it as an absolutely unique work of art. However, a certain German was particularly annoyed that Madame de Staël expressed such an extraordinarily favorable opinion of it.[4] I would just like to read you this man's opinion, so that you see that about such things that have to be judged individually there can be different opinions from those you may consider at this moment to be the only opinions one can possibly have of Goethe's *Faust*.

This critical opinion was written down in 1822 by a certain Franz von Spaun.[5] Here is his criticism of Goethe's *Faust*, which begins right away with the "Prologue in Heaven:"

[Right from the Prologue] we see that Herr von Goethe is a very bad versifier and that the Prologue itself is a true sample of how one ought not to write verse.

Past ages show nothing that can compare with this Prologue for presumptuous paltriness.... But I must be brief, for I have undertaken a long and, alas, wearisome piece of work. I have to point out to the reader that this notorious *Faust* enjoys an usurped and unmerited renown that it owes only to the pernicious *esprit de corps* of an *Associato obscurorum vitorum*.... It is not because I wish to rival this renown that I am compelled to vent the sarcasm of harsh criticism upon Goethe's *Faust*. I do not travel by his path to Parnassus, and should have been glad if he had enriched our German language with a masterpiece.... Among the multitudes who applaud, my voice may be extinguished, yet it is enough for me to have done my best; and if I succeed in converting even one reader and recalling him from the worship of this atrocity, I shall not grudge my thankless labor.... The wretched Faust speaks an incomprehensible gibberish, in the most atrocious rhyme of any fifth grade student. My teacher would have thrashed me soundly if I had made inferior verses such as the following:

Oh, broad bright moon, if this might be
The last of the nights of agony,
The countless midnights of toil and ache,
I've pass'd at this dreary desk awake!

galimatas

Concerning the baseness of the diction, the paltriness of the verse, I will henceforth be silent; what the reader has seen is sufficient proof that the author, as far as the construction of his verse is concerned, cannot stand comparison with the mediocre poets of the old school. . . .

Mephistopheles himself realized even before the contract was signed that Faust was possessed by a devil. We, however, think he belongs in a lunatic asylum rather than in Hell, with all his accessories—hands and feet, head and posterior. Of sublime galimatias, of nonsense in high-faluting words, many poets have given us samples, but Goethe's nonsense or galimatias might be called a popular galimatias, a *genre nouveau*, for it is presented in the commonest, most atrocious language. . . .

The more I think about this long litany of nonsense, the more probable it seems to me that there must have been a wager to the effect that if a celebrated man permitted himself to patch together the dullest, most boring nonsense, a legion of literary simpletons and deluded readers would find deep wisdom and great beauty in this insipid nonsense and know how to expound upon it. Famous men have this in common with Prince Piribinker and the immortal Dalai Lama that their rubbish is served up as sweetmeats and revered as relics. If this was Herr von Goethe's intention, he has won the wager. . . .

There may well be some intentions behind *Faust*, yet a good poet does not hurl them at his readers; he should know the art of presenting and illuminating them properly. A richer theme for poetry than this is not easy to find, and people will be cross with him for bungling it so miserably. . . .

This diarrhea of undigested ideas is not caused by an excessive flow of healthy fluids but by a relaxation of the floodgates of the mind, and is an indication of a weak constitution. There are people from whom bad verse flows like water, but this *incontinentia urinae poeticae,* this *diabetes mellitus* of lame verses never afflicts a good poet. . . . If Goethe's genius has freed itself from all fetters, the flood of his ideas cannot break through the dams of art, for they have already been broken through. Yet although we do not disapprove of an author's breaking away from the conventional rules of composition, he must still hold sacred the laws of sound human reason, of grammar and rhythm. Even in dramas where magic plays a part, he is only allowed the machinery of hypothesis, and he must remain faithful to this. He must make a good plot with a knot to be unraveled and the magic must lead to grand results. In the case of *Faust* the outcome is to seduce the victims to dastardly crimes, and his seducer does not need magic; everything he does any matchmaking scoundrel could have done just as well without witchcraft. He is as stingy as a miser, not using the hidden treasures at his command.

In short, a miserable wretch who might learn something from Lessing's *Marinelli.* Therefore, in the name of sound human reason I quash the opinion of Madame de Staël in favor of the aforesaid *Faust* and condemn it, not to Hell, which might be cooled off by this frigid production that even has a wintry effect on the devil, but to be thrown into the sewer of Parnassus. And by rights.

As you see, this judgment was actually passed upon *Faust* at one time, and the context in which the man passed it does not at all prove him to be entirely dishonest, but someone who believed what he wrote. Now imagine what would have happened if this man, who said that his own fifth grade teacher would have kept him from writing such rubbish as *Faust,* had himself become a school teacher and passed on this nonsense to a great number of boys. These boys might in their turn have become teachers and remembered something of this verdict on *Faust*. Just think of all the speculations you can make regarding all the karmic damage this person might have done by means of his judgment.

However, I am less concerned about that than about the fact that it is difficult to form a true, permanent judgment concerning events possessing their own intrinsic value. I have emphasized in some of my lectures that many a great personality of the nineteenth century will no longer be considered great in centuries to come, whereas people who have been quite forgotten will by that time be regarded as very significant indeed. Time puts such things right. I only wanted to point out how extremely difficult it is to form a judgment about an event needing to be looked at on its own merit.

We must now ask why that causes us such difficulty. We shall begin our reflections by seeing the critic as a different person from the one who is being judged. Nowadays we would say that the people who even in those days considered Goethe's *Faust* to be a great work of art and in a certain way judged it objectively eliminated themselves, so to speak. The man who wrote what I have just been reading to you did not eliminate himself. How do we arrive at judgments that are not objective? People judge without objectivity so often that it never occurs to them to ask why they do this. They do it because of the forces of sympathy and antipathy. Without sympathy and antipathy our judgments would never be other than objective.

Sympathy and antipathy are necessary in order to obscure the objectivity of judgment. Does this mean they are bad, however, and that we ought immediately to do away with them? We need only reflect a little to find that this is not so. For no sooner do we engross ourselves in Goethe's *Faust* than we like it and develop more and more feelings of sympathy towards it. We must have the possibility to develop sympathy. And after all, if we were unable to develop antipathy we would not arrive at an absolutely correct judgment of the man whose opinion we have just heard. For I imagine some antipathetic feelings against the man may have arisen in you, and they could well be justified.

But there again we see that it depends on not accepting these things as absolute but considering them in their whole context. It is not merely that human beings are brought to feelings of sympathy and antipathy by outer things but that we carry sympathy and antipathy into life. We bring our sympathy and antipathy to meet the things themselves, so that they do not work upon us but upon our sympathy and antipathy. What does this mean? I approach an object or a process accompanied by my sympathy and antipathy. Naturally the man I was speaking about did not exactly bring along his antipathy to *Faust* but he brought the kind of feelings that made him see *Faust* as antipathetic. He judged absolutely according to his instincts.

What does this signify? It means that sympathy and antipathy, to start with, are only words for real spiritual facts. And the real spiritual facts are the deeds of Lucifer and Ahriman. In a certain way Lucifer is in every expression of sympathy and Ahriman in every expression of antipathy. By letting ourselves be carried through the world by sympathy and antipathy, we are letting ourselves be carried through the world by Lucifer and Ahriman. Only we must not fall into the mistake I have often described and say yet again "We must flee from both Lucifer and Ahriman! We want to become good. So we must avoid Lucifer and Ahriman, avoid them at all costs! We must drive them away, right away!" For then we should also have to leave the world. For just as there can be both positive and negative electricity and not

39

only the balance between them, so we encounter Lucifer and Ahriman wherever we go. It all depends on how we relate to them. These two forces must be there. The important thing is that we always bring them into balance in life. For instance, without Lucifer art would not exist. What matters is that we create art that is not purely luciferic.

Thus it is a matter of becoming aware that when we confront the world with sympathy and antipathy, Lucifer and Ahriman are at work in us. That is to say, we must be able to allow Lucifer and Ahriman really to be active in us. But while we are conscious that they are at work in us, we must nevertheless acquire the capacity to confront things objectively. This we can do only if we consider not merely how we judge external things and events in the world outside us, but also consider how we judge ourselves in the world. And this "judging ourselves in the world" leads us a step further into the question and the whole complex of questions we started with. We can form a judgment of ourselves in the world only if we apply to ourselves a uniform method of consideration. We must now consider this problem.

We look out upon nature. On the one hand, we see rigid necessity; one thing arising from another. We look at our own deeds and believe that they are subject only to freedom and are connected solely with guilt and atonement and so on. Both views are one-sided. In what follows it will be shown that each view is one-sided because neither correctly estimates the position of Lucifer and Ahriman. If we look at ourselves as human beings existing here on the physical plane, we cannot look into our own souls and see only what is taking place in the immediate present. If each one of us were to ask ourselves what is taking place within us right now, it would certainly be a piece of insight into our-selves. Yet this insight would be far from giving us everything we required even for superficial self-knowl-edge.

Without hurting anyone's feelings, of course, let us consider all of us here: I who am speaking and you who are listening. I would not be able to speak as I do if it were not for everything that has previously happened in my present life and in other incarnations. Looking only at what I am saying to you now would produce a very one-sided kind of self-knowledge. But without hurting anyone's feelings it must be obvious that each one of you listens differently, and understands and feels what I say slightly differently. That goes without saying. In fact your understanding is in accordance with your life up to now and your previous incarnations. If each one of you did not grasp differently what is being said, you would not really be human beings.

But that leads much further. It leads to the recogni-tion of a duality in ourselves. Just think for a moment that when you pass judgment, you do it in a certain way. Let us take a random example. If you see one thing or another, a play directed by Max Reinhardt, for exam-ple, you say, "It is charming!" while someone else says "That is the ruin of all art!"[6] I am certainly not criticizing either opinion just now. It is possible for one person to say this and another that. On what does it depend that one person has a different opinion from another? That depends again on what is already in them, upon the assumptions with which they approach matters.

But if you think about these assumptions, you will be able to say "At one time these assumptions did not exist." What you saw when you were eighteen, for in-stance, or learned at the age of thirteen, enters into your present judgments. It has become part of your whole thinking, resides in you, and contributes to your judgment. Everyone can of course perceive this in himself if he wishes to do so. It contributes to your judgment. Ask yourself whether you can change what is now in you, or whether you can tear it out of yourself. Think about it for a moment! If we could tear it out, we would be taking away the whole of our life up to now; we would be obliterating ourselves. We can no more get rid of our previous resolutions and decisions than we can give ourselves another nose if we do not like what we see in the mirror.

It is obvious that you cannot obliterate your past. Yet if you wish to rise early in the morning, you see, a resolution is always necessary. This resolution, however, is really dependent upon the prior conditions of your present incarnation. It depends on other things as well. If we say it depends on this or that, does that detract from the fact that I have to resolve to get up? This decision to get up may be so faint that we do not notice it at all, but at least a faint resolve to get up has to be there, that is to say, getting up must be a free deed.

I knew a man who belonged for a time to our Society and who is a good illustration of this, for he actually never wanted to get up. He suffered terribly because of it, and often deplored it. He said, "I simply cannot get up! Unless something occurs in the way of an external necessity to make me rise from my bed, I would stay there forever." He confessed this openly, for he found it a terrible temptation in life not to want to get up. From this you can easily see that it really is a free deed. And although certain prior conditions have been laid down in us which suggest one or another motive, it does not prevent our doing a free deed in the particular instance.

In a certain way it is like this: Some people drag themselves out of bed with the help of strong determination, while others enjoy getting up. We could easily say that this shows us that the existing prior conditions signify that the one was brought up well and the other badly. We can see a certain necessity there, yet it is always a free decision. Thus we see in one and the same fact, in the fact of getting up, free will and necessity interwoven, thoroughly interwoven. One and the same thing contains both freedom and necessity. And I beg you to note well that, rightly considered, we cannot dispute whether a person is free or unfree in a certain matter, but we can only say that first of all freedom and necessity are intermingled in every human deed.

How does this happen? We shall not progress with our spiritual science unless we realize that we have to consider things both from the human and the cosmic standpoint. Why is this so? It is because what works in us as necessity—I will now say something relatively simple yet of tremendous significance—what we regard as necessity belongs to the past. What works in us as necessity must always be from the past. We must have experienced something, and this experience must have been stored up in our souls. It is then within our soul and continues to work there as necessity.

You can now say that everybody bears his past within him, and this means bearing a necessity within him. What belongs to the present does not yet work as necessity, otherwise there would be no free deed in the immediate present. But the past works into the present and combines with freedom. Because the past works on, freedom and necessity are intimately connected in one and the same deed.

Thus if we really look into ourselves, we will see that necessity exists not only outside us in nature but also within ourselves. When we look at this latter kind of

— to create the future

43

necessity, we have to look at our past. This is an extremely important point of view for a spiritual scientist. He learns to understand the connection between past and necessity. Then he begins to examine nature, and finds necessity there. And in examining natural phenomena he realizes that all the necessities the natural scientist finds in nature are the result of past events. What is nature as a whole, the whole realm of nature with its necessity?

We cannot answer that unless we look for the answer on the basis of spiritual science. We are now living in earth existence, a condition which was preceded by the moon, sun and Saturn conditions. In the Saturn condition, as you see in *Occult Science*, the planet did not look like the earth does now but entirely differently.[7] If you examine Saturn, you will see that then everything was still of a thoughtlike nature. Stones did not yet fall to the ground. Dense physical matter did not exist as yet. Everything came from the activity of warmth. This state is similar to what goes on within the human being itself. Everything is soul activity, thoughts that divine spirits have left behind. And they have remained in existence.

All of present nature that you understand with its necessity was once in a state of freedom, a free deed of the gods. Only because it is past, because what developed on Saturn, sun, and moon has come to us in the same way as our childhood thoughts continue to work in us, the thoughts of the gods during Saturn, sun, and moon continue their existence on earth. And because they are past thoughts, they appear to us as necessity.

If you now put your hand on a solid object, what does that mean? It means that what is in the solid object was once being thought in the long distant past, and has remained in the same way as your childhood thoughts have remained in you. If you look at your

past, regarding past activities as something living, you see nature in the process of becoming within you. Just as what you now think and say is not a necessity but is free, so earth's present state was once free in earlier stages of existence. Freedom continually evolves, and what is left behind becomes necessity. If we were to see what is taking place in nature now, it would not occur to us to see it as a necessity. What we see of nature is only what has been left behind. What is happening now in nature is spiritual, and we do not see that.

This gives human self-knowledge a very special cosmic significance. We think a thought. It is now within us. Certainly we might also *not* think it. But if we think it, it remains in our soul, where it becomes an activity of the past. It now works on as a necessity, a delicate, insubstantial necessity, and not dense matter like outer nature because we are human beings, not gods. We can perceive only the inner nature that remains in us as memory and is operative in what are necessities for us. But our current thoughts will become external nature in the coming Jupiter and Venus conditions. They will then be the external environment. And what we now see as nature was once the thoughts of the gods.

Nowadays we speak of angels, archangels, archai, and so on. They were thinking in the past, just as we are thinking today. And what they thought has remained as their memory, and it is this memory we now perceive. We can only perceive within us what we remember during earth existence. But inwardly it has become nature. What the gods thought during earlier planetary conditions has been externalized and we see it as external nature.

It is true, profoundly true, that as long as we are earthly human beings we think. We send our thoughts down into our soul life. There they become the beginning of a natural world. But they remain in us. Yet when the Jupiter existence comes, they will come forth. And what we are thinking today, in fact all that we experience, will then be the external world. The external world we will then look down upon from a higher level will be what is now our inner world. What is experienced at one time in freedom changes into necessity.

These are very, very important aspects, and only when we see the world in this way will we be able to understand the real course of historical events and the significance of today's events. For these lead us directly to the point where we always pursue the path from subjectivity to objectivity. Strictly speaking, we can be subjective only in the present. As soon as the present is over, and we have pushed the subjective elements down into our soul life, they acquire independent existence, though at first only within us. As we continue living with other thoughts, the earlier thoughts live on, only in us, of course. For the time being we still house them. But this covering will some day fall away.

In the spiritual realm matters are very different. So you must look at events, such as the hypothetical one I gave you, from this different point of view. Looked at from outside, a boulder fell and buried a party of people. But that was only the external expression of something that happened in the spiritual world, this latter event being the other half of the experience and existing just as objectively as the first one.

This is what I wanted to present to you today, showing how freedom and necessity play into one another in world evolution and in the evolution in which we are involved as living beings; how we are interwoven with the world, and how we ourselves are daily, hourly, becoming what nature shows us externally. Our past, while within us, is already a piece of nature. We pro-

46

gress beyond this piece of nature by evolving further, just as the gods progressed in their evolution beyond their nature stage and became the higher hierarchies.

This is only one of the ways, of which there are many, that ought to show us again and again that nothing taking place on the physical plane can be judged solely according to its physical aspect, but should be judged based on the knowledge that it has a hidden spiritual content in addition to the physical one. As sure as our physical body has an etheric body in it, everything perceived by the senses has a supersensible part underlying it. Therefore, we must conclude that we are really regarding the world in a very incomplete way if we examine it solely according to what it presents to our eyes and according to what takes place externally, for while something quite different is taking place externally, inwardly something can be happening spiritually that belongs to the outer event and is of immensely greater significance than what is presented to our senses. What the souls of the people who were buried under the boulder experienced in the spiritual world may be infinitely more important than what happened physically. The occurrence has something to do with the future of those souls, as we shall see.

Let us interrupt these thoughts at this point today and continue them next Sunday. My aim today was to bring your thoughts and ideas into the direction that will show you that we can only acquire correct concepts of freedom and necessity, guilt and atonement, and so on, if we add the spiritual aspect to the physical one.

Lecture III

January 30, 1916

To continue last week's study I shall begin with a kind of hypothetical case. Where the deepest riddles of human existence are concerned the best way to avoid abstraction and to get close to reality is to give examples. My example will of course apply to every possible level of life. So let us begin with a hypothetical example.

Let us imagine we are in a school, a school of three classes, with three teachers and a headmaster. These three teachers differ tremendously in character and temperament. It is the beginning of a new school year. The headmaster discusses the coming year with his teachers. First of all it is the turn of the first teacher. The headmaster asks him what preparations he intends to make and what he thinks is the best way to proceed in the coming year. The teacher replies, "Well, during the holidays I noted down carefully all the areas where the pupils did not meet my expectations, areas that I had obviously not prepared well. And I have drawn up a new plan for next year containing all the things which I am sure were successful and got across to the children. All the work I will give them next year consists of the things that came off best last year and have proved successful." A further question from the headmaster produced a complete schedule the teacher had made of the subject matter. He could also stipulate what work he would give the pupils to do in school and what would be set as homework in the course of the year. All his themes, both for schoolwork and homework, had

49

been chosen from careful scanning of the previous year. The headmaster was very satisfied and said "You are doubtless a conscientious teacher, and I reckon you will achieve excellent results with your class."

The second teacher also said, "I have gone through the whole curriculum I covered with my pupils last year and noted everything I did wrong. I have arranged the new schedule avoiding all the mistakes I made before." And he, too, was able to show the headmaster a curriculum containing all the subjects he was going to give the pupils for schoolwork and homework in the course of the year, basing it on the experience of his last year's mistakes. The headmaster said, "The teacher I have just spoken to noted all the instances where he had achieved excellence, and tried to plan his curriculum accordingly, whereas you have endeavored to avoid mistakes. It can be done either way. I am assured that you will achieve excellent results with your class. I see with a certain satisfaction that I have teachers in my school who review their past achievements and let the wisdom of self-knowledge guide their future steps." You see, a teacher who knows his priorities is bound to make a good impression on a headmaster.

Then it was the third teacher's turn. He said, "During the holidays I, too, have thought a lot about what happened in my class last year. I have tried to study the character of my pupils and have done a kind of review of what has taken place in the various individuals." "Well," said the headmaster, "you will also have seen the mistakes you made and the things you did well, and will have been able to draw up a schedule for the coming year." "No," replied the teacher. "I have certainly made mistakes; and some things I have done well. But I have only studied the pupils' characters and what has taken place there. I have not thought especially about whether I made any particular mistakes, or whether this or that was particularly good. I did not do that. I accepted that things had to happen the way they did. So I have just observed what I believe had to happen out of a certain necessity. The pupils had their various dispositions, and these I observed carefully. I too have a definite disposition, and the interaction of our different natures produced its own results. I cannot say more than that."

"Well," said the headmaster, "you seem to be a very self-satisfied person. Have you at least drawn up a schedule, and worked out the subjects you will give your pupils as schoolwork and homework during the year?" "No," he answered, "I have not done that." "Well, what do you intend to do with your class?" To this the teacher replied, "I will see what kinds of pupils I will have this year. And I believe I will be able to size this up better than last year, as each year I have always studied the previous year's characters during the holidays. But I cannot possibly know yet what they will be like next year. Only time will tell." "Well, are you not intending to plan subjects for schoolwork and homework?" "Yes, but not until I have seen what my pupils' capacities are like. I will try to set the work accordingly." "Well, really," said the headmaster, "we would be thoroughly at sea in that case. We can hardly allow such things to happen."

But there was nothing to be done. The headmaster had to agree to it, and the school year got under way. The headmaster inspected the school frequently. He saw the first two teachers doing exceedingly well, but with the third he always found that things were not on a good footing. There was no certainty, he said, one never really knew what would happen the following month. And it went on like this throughout the year.

Then came the time for the report cards. From those of the first two teachers the headmaster was satisfied that they had been very successful. Of course, some of the pupils in their classes failed too, and others passed, but it all happened as expected. According to the report cards, the third teacher's results were no worse. Yet other people had come to the conclusion over the year that he was very lenient. While the other teachers were strict, he was so lenient that he frequently made allowances, and the headmaster was convinced that the third teacher's class had come out the worst.

Then the next year came. The holidays were over, and at the start of the school year the first two teachers spoke as before, and the third, too. Things happened similarly, with the school inspector also coming occasionally, and, of course, he noticed what the headmaster had as it were prepared him to see, namely that the first two teachers were very good, and the third only second-rate. It could not be otherwise. I hardly need mention that after a few years the two good teachers were nominated for decorations, and the headmaster received an even higher one. That is a matter of secondary importance, isn't it?

Some time later the following thing happened. The headmaster left the school and another came at the beginning of the year. He also discussed with his three teachers what their plans were, and so on, and each of the teachers answered in a similar way as before. Then the headmaster said, "There is certainly quite a difference between your methods. And I believe the first two gentlemen ought to take a little guidance from the third teacher." "What!" said the first two gentlemen. "The previous headmaster always said that he ought to take guidance from us!" "I do not think so," said the new head. "It seems to me that the first two should adapt to the third." But they could not very well emulate him, for they could not see how anyone could possibly foresee what would happen in the coming year if he groped about as blindly as that teacher did. They just could not imagine it.

In the meantime the former headmaster, because of his insight into proper school administration, had himself become a school inspector, and was most astonished at the views his successor was expressing about the school he knew so well. How could such a thing happen? And he said, "The third teacher never told me anything except 'I must first see what the pupils are like, then I can form my schedule from week to week.' But that way you cannot look ahead at all! It is quite impossible to manage if you cannot anticipate a single thing." To which the present headmaster replied, "Yes, but look, I have actually asked my teachers about their different ways of looking ahead. The first two gentlemen always say 'I know for certain that on February 25 next year I will present such and such items of schoolwork. I can say in detail what will be happening, and I know for certain that I will be talking about such and such a subject at Easter.' The third teacher says 'I do not know for certain what I will be doing at Easter, nor do I know what schoolwork I will set in February. I will set the work according to the kind of pupils I have.' And by that he meant that he can in a certain way foresee that all will be well. And," said the new headmaster, "I actually agree with him entirely. You cannot know until afterwards whether your resolves have been entirely successful. It depends on the attitude you have to the previous year; if you study the character of last year's pupils, you acquire greater capacities to understand the character of the new pupils. I appreciate that more can be achieved this way."

"Yes, but you still cannot know anything in advance! Everything is in the realm of uncertainty. How can you predetermine anything for the whole school year?" asked the former headmaster. "You cannot anticipate anything. But you must be able to look ahead a little bit, if you want to make proper plans." "You *can* foresee that things will go well," said the new headmaster, "if you join forces as it were with the spirit at work in the pupils, and have a certain faith in it. If you, so to speak, pledge yourself to this and depend upon it, then even if you cannot anticipate the school work you will be presenting in February, you will know that it will be the right work." "Yes, but you cannot foresee anything with certainty, and everything remains vague," said the school inspector, to which the new headmaster replied, "You know, I once studied the sort of thing people call spiritual science. And I still remember from this that beings on a much higher level than human beings are actually supposed to have acted in this way in much more important affairs. For at the beginning of the Bible it says 'And God made light.' And only after he made the light does it say 'And he saw that it was good.'" To this the inspector had nothing suitable to say.

Things continued in the same way for a time. There are few headmasters like the second one I chose as a hypothetical example, aren't there? I could call him hypothetical to the second degree, for even with it being a hypothesis it is hypothetical to assume a headmaster like that. Therefore he was dismissed very soon, and another one more like the inspector was appointed. And things ran their course until one day it went so far that the completely "undecorated" teacher was driven away from the school in disgrace and another of the same style as the first two was appointed in his place. The outcome could not possibly have been any different at the time, for in all the yearbooks and personnel files it was recorded what great progress had been achieved by the first two teachers, while of the third one it was recorded that he sent out only poor students from the school for the simple reason that he made allowances; otherwise all his pupils would have failed. There was absolutely nothing that could be done about a person like this third teacher.

Many years passed. By chance a very unusual event followed. The headmaster who had been dismissed tried to go more deeply into how matters had turned out with the two teachers who had always practiced strict self-observation, for example, with the one who noted the subjects that yielded fewer successes and selected the more successful ones. The former headmaster also wanted to know what the second and the third teachers had achieved. He even followed up what their pupils had achieved under other teachers, and he discovered that with different teachers the third teacher's pupils made much less progress than those of the first two. But the former headmaster did not stop there. He went even further into the matter and traced the subsequent life of the former pupils of these teachers. He then discovered that those taught by the first two teachers, with a few exceptions naturally, had all become respectable citizens, yet they had achieved nothing outstanding. Among the pupils taught by the third teacher, however, were people of considerable importance, who accomplished things of far greater significance than the pupils of the others.

He was able to prove these things in this particular case. But it made no special impression on people, for they said, "We cannot always wait to follow up the pupils' whole subsequent lives! That is impossible, isn't it? And that is not the point, anyway."

Now why am I telling you all this? There is an important difference between the first two teachers and the third. Throughout the holidays, the first two teachers kept focusing their attention on the way they had done their work the previous year. The third teacher did not do this, for he had the feeling that it had to happen as it did. When the headmaster, the first one, kept telling him again and again, "But you won't have any idea how to avoid mistakes next year, or how to do the right thing, if you don't study what you did well last year," he did not answer immediately, for he did not feel like explaining this to him. But afterwards he thought to himself, "Well, even if I did know what mistakes happened in the course of the work my pupils and I did together, I will after all have different pupils this year, and our working together is not affected by the mistakes made last year. I have to work with new pupils."

In short, the first two teachers were wholly entrenched in a dead element, while the third teacher entered into what was alive. You could also say that the first two teachers always dealt with the past, the third teacher with the immediate present. He did not brood over the past, but said, "Of necessity it had to happen as it did according to the conditions that prevailed."

The point is that if things are judged in a superficial way according to external judgments, one can indeed go astray where actual facts are concerned. Because if you were to do things the way the first teachers did them you would be judging the present according to what is dead and gone and what ought to be allowed to remain so. The third teacher took what was still alive from the past, arriving at it by simply studying character, and made himself more perfect by doing so; in fact, he did it with this in view. For he told himself, "If I can make myself more efficient in this way, the greater capacities I thus acquire will help me achieve what I have to do in the future."

The first two teachers were somewhat superstitious about the past and told themselves, "Past mistakes must be avoided in the future and evident good qualities must be used." But they did this in a dead way. They had no intention of enhancing their abilities but only of making their decisions according to outer observation. They did not have the wish to be effective as a result of working in a living way on themselves; they thought the only means to gain anything for the future was observation and its results.

In accordance with spiritual science we have to say that the first teacher, who investigated so carefully the good qualities he had established in the past and wanted to incorporate them in his future work, acted in an ahrimanic way. It was an ahrimanic approach. He clung to the past, and out of personal egotism looked with complacent satisfaction at everything he had done well and prided himself on it.

The second teacher's character was governed more by luciferic forces. He brooded over his mistakes and told himself, "I must avoid these mistakes." He did not say, "The things that happened were necessary, and had to happen like that," but said, "I have made mistakes." There is always something egotistic about it when we would like to have been better than we actually were, and tell ourselves we made mistakes that ought to have been avoided and that we must now avoid. We are clinging to the past, like Lucifer does, who, on a spiritual level, brings past happenings into the present. That is thinking in a luciferic way.

The third teacher was, I would say, filled with the forces of divine beings who are progressing in a normal way, whose correct divine principle is expressed right

57

at the beginning of the Bible, where we are told that the Elohim first of all create and then they see that their creation was good. They do not look upon it egotistically as though they were superior beings for having made a good creation, but they admit that it is good in order to continue creating. They incorporate it into their evolution. They live and work in the element of life.

What is important is that we realize that we ourselves are living beings and a part of a living world. If we realize this, we will not criticize the gods, the Elohim, for instance. For anyone wishing to set his own wisdom above that of the gods might say, "If gods are supposed to be gods, could they not see that the light would be good? Those gods do not even sound like prophets to me. If I were a god, I would of course only create light if I knew beforehand what light was like, and did not have to wait till later to see that it was good." But that is human wisdom being placed above divine wisdom.

In a certain way the third teacher also saw what would come about, but he saw it in a living way in that he surrendered himself to the spirit of becoming, the spirit of development. When he said, "By incorporating what I have gained through the study of last year's characters and not focusing on the mistakes I made of necessity, simply because I was as I was, nor applying criticism to what I encountered as my own past, I have enhanced my capacities and acquired in addition a better understanding for my new pupils." And he realized that the first two teachers were considering their pupils merely in the light of what they had done the previous year, which they could not even estimate properly. So he could say, "I am quite certain I will give my pupils the right schoolwork in four weeks time, and I have every confidence in my prediction."

The others were better prophets. They could actually

say "I will present the schoolwork I have written down; I will give them that for sure." But that was a foreseeing of facts, not a foreseeing of the course of the forces of movement. We must hold very firmly to this distinction. Prediction as such is not impossible. But predicting in detail what will happen when these details are interwoven with a living element that is to work out of itself is possible only when we consider the phenomena that Lucifer and Ahriman carry over from the present into the future.

We are gradually getting closer to the big problem occupying us in these lectures on freedom and necessity. However, as this particular problem affects so profoundly the whole matter of world processes and human action, we must not fail to look at all the difficulties. For instance, we must realize clearly that when we look back at events that have happened and in which we have been involved, we look at them as necessity. The moment we know all the circumstances, we consider the events as necessity. There is no doubt about the fact that we look upon what has happened as a necessity.

But at the same time we have to ask, "Can we really, as so often happens, always find the causes of events in what immediately preceded them?" In a certain way natural science has to look at what has just happened to see what will happen next. If I carry out an experiment, I have to realize that the cause of what takes place later obviously lies in what took place previously. But that does not mean at all that this principle applies to every process in the world. For we might very easily deceive ourselves about the connection between cause and effect if we were to look for it along the lines of what comes first and what comes later. I would like to explain this with a comparison.

When we penetrate external reality with our senses, we can say, "Because this thing is like this, then the other must be like that." But if we apply this to every process, we very often arrive at the error I want to illustrate. For the sake of simplicity let us take a man driving himself in a cart, an example I have often taken. We see a horse with a cart behind it and a man sitting in it holding the reins. We look at it and quite naturally say that the horse is pulling and the man is being pulled. The man is being taken wherever the horse takes him. That is quite obvious. Therefore the horse is the cause of the man's being pulled along. The pulling being done by the horse is the cause, and the fact of the man being pulled is the effect. Fair enough! But you all know very well that that is not so; that the man sitting up there driving himself is leading the horse where he wants him to go. Although the horse is pulling him, it is taking him where he wants to go.

Such mistakes happen often when we judge purely externally, on the basis of happenings on the physical plane. Let us look once more at the hypothetical examples I gave you a few days ago, in which a party of people set out for a drive, got into the coach, but the driver was delayed, and they were five minutes behind time. Therefore they arrive beneath an overhanging boulder at the moment it falls, and it crushes them all. Now if we trace the cause on the physical plane, we can naturally say, "This happened first and then that and then the other." And we will arrive at something. But in this case we could easily make the same mistake we make if we say the horse pulls the driver wherever it wants and overlook the fact that the driver is leading the horse. Perhaps we make this mistake because the controlling force in this case is possibly to be found in

60

the spiritual world. If we merely trace events on the physical plane we really judge in the sense of saying the man is going where the horse takes him. However, if we penetrate to the hidden forces at work in the occurrence, we see that events were directed toward that point and that the driver's belated arrival was actually part of the whole complex of circumstances. It was all necessary, but not necessary in the way one might believe if one merely traces events on the physical plane.

Again, if you believe you can find the cause by assuming it to be what has happened immediately beforehand, the following might happen. Seen externally it looks like this. Two people meet. We now proceed in the proper scientific manner. The two have met, so we enquire where they were during the hour before they met, where they were an hour before that, and how they set out to meet one another. We can now trace over a certain length of time how one thing has always led to another, and how the two were brought together. Someone else who does not concern himself with this sort of thing hears by chance that the two people had arranged five days beforehand that they would meet, and he says, "They have met because they planned to do so."

Here you have an opportunity to see that the cause for something is not necessarily connected with the immediately preceding event. In fact if we break off looking for the chain of causes before we come to the right link in the chain, we shall never find it, for after all we can only follow the chain of causes up to a certain point. In nature, too, we can only follow it up to a certain point, particularly in the case of phenomena involving human beings. And if we do this, and go from one event to the other, tracing what was before that and before that again, and imagine we will find the cause this way, we are obviously laying ourselves open to error, to deception.

You have to grasp this with what you have acquired from spiritual science. Suppose a person carries out some action on the physical plane. We see him doing it. If we want to limit our observations to the physical plane, we will look into his behavior prior to the action. If we go further, we will look into how he was brought up. We might also follow the modern fashion of looking at his heredity, and so on. However, let us assume that into this action on the physical plane something has entered that is only to be found in the life of that person between his previous death and rebirth. This means that we must break off the chain of causes at his birth and pass over to something that resembles the prior arrangement made by the two people in my example. For what I have just described may have been predetermined hundreds of years before in the life between the last death and the birth into the present life. What was experienced then enters into our present actions and resolves.

Thus it is inevitable that unless we include the sphere of the spirit, we cannot find the causes of human actions at all, certainly not here on the physical plane, and that a search for causes similar to the way people look for causes of events in outer nature may go very wrong.

Yet if we look more closely at the way human action is interwoven with world processes, we will arrive at a satisfactory way of looking at things, even of looking at what we call freedom, although we have to admit that necessity exists also. But what we call the search for causes is perhaps for the time being limited most of all by the fact that on the physical plane one cannot penetrate to the place where causes originate.

Now we come to something else that has to be considered. The two concepts freedom and necessity are extremely difficult to grasp and even more difficult to reconcile. It is not for nothing that philosophy for the most part fails when it comes to the problem of freedom and necessity. This is largely due to the fact that human beings have not looked fairly and squarely at the difficulties these problems entail. That is why I am trying so hard to focus in these lectures on all the possible difficulties.

When we look at human activities, the first thing we see everywhere is the thread of necessity. For it would be biased to say that every human action is a product of freedom. Let me give you another hypothetical example. Imagine someone growing up. Through the way he is growing up, it can be shown that all the circumstances have gone in the direction of making him a postman, a country postman, who has to go out into the country every morning with the mail and deliver letters. He does the same round every day. I expect you will all agree that a certain necessity can be found in this whole process. If we look at all that happened to this lad in his childhood and take into account everything that had its effect on his life, we will certainly see that all these things combined to make him a mailman. So that as soon as there was a vacant position he was pushed into it of necessity, at which point freedom certainly ceased to exist, for of course he cannot alter the addresses of the letters he gets. There is now an external necessity that dictates the doors at which he has to call. So we certainly see a great deal of necessity in what he has to do.

But now let us imagine another person, younger perhaps. I will assume him to be younger so that I can describe what I want to describe without your objecting too strongly to the way he behaves. Well then, another, younger person, not out of idleness but just because he is still so young, makes up his mind to go with the mailman every morning and accompany him on his round. He gets up in good time every morning, joins the postman and takes part in all the details of the round for a considerable while.

Now it is obvious that we cannot talk of necessity in the case of the second fellow in the same sense as we can of the first. For everything the first fellow does must happen, whereas nothing the second fellow does has to be done. He could have stayed at home any day, and exactly the same things would have happened from an objective standpoint. This is obvious, isn't it? So we could say that the first man does everything out of necessity and the second everything out of freedom. We can very well say this, and yet in one sense they are both doing the same thing. We might even imagine the following. A morning comes when the second fellow does not want to get up. He could quite well have stayed in bed, but he gets up all the same because he is now used to doing so. He does with a certain necessity what he is doing out of freedom. We see freedom and necessity virtually overlapping.

If we study the way our second self lives in us—the one I told you about in the public lecture,[1] our actual soul nature, which will pass through the gate of death—it could, after all, be compared with someone accompanying the outer human being in the physical world. An ordinary materialistic monist would think this was a dreadful thing to say. But we know that a materialistic monist takes the view that people are terrible dualists if they believe water consists of hydrogen and oxygen. For them everything must be undifferentiated. They think it is nonsense to say that the monon "water" consists of hydrogen and oxygen. But we must not let monism deceive us.

The crux of the matter is that what we are in life really consists of two parts that come together from two different directions, and these two parts can indeed be compared with the oxygen and hydrogen in water. For our external physical nature comes through the line of heredity, bringing not only physical characteristics with it but also social status. It is not just our particular form with its nose, color of hair, and so on that we get from our father and mother, but our social position is also predestined through our ancestors' positions in life. Thus not only the appearance of our physical body, the strength of our muscles and so on, but our position in society and everything pertaining to the physical plane comes through the line of heredity from one generation to the other.

Our individual being originating in the spiritual world comes from a different direction, and at first it has nothing to do with all the forces in the stream of heredity through the generations, but brings with it causes that may have been laid down in us centuries before, and unites them on a spiritual level with the causes residing in the stream of heredity. Two beings come together. And in fact we can only judge the matter rightly if we regard this second being coming from the spiritual world and uniting with the physical being as a kind of companion to the first one. That is why I chose the example of the companion who joins us in everything. Our soul being in a certain sense joins us in the external events in a similar way.

The other person accompanying the postman did it all voluntarily. This cannot be denied. We could certainly look for causes, but compared with the necessity that binds the first postman the causes for the second man's actions lie in the realm of freedom. He did it all voluntarily. But look closely and you will see that one thing follows with necessity from this freedom. You will not deny that if the second person had accompanied the first person long enough, he would doubtlessly have become a good mailman. He would have easily been able to do what the man he accompanied did. He would even have been able to do it better, because he would avoid certain mistakes. But if the first fellow had not made these mistakes, the second man would not have become aware of them. We cannot possibly imagine that it would be of any use if the second fellow were to think about the first one's mistakes. If we think in a living way, we will consider this to be an utterly futile occupation. By specifically *not thinking* about the mistakes but joining in the work in a living way and just observing the proceedings as a whole, he will acquire them through life and will as a matter of course not make these mistakes.

This is just how it is with the being that accompanies us within. If this being can rise to the perception that what we have done is necessary, that we have accompanied it and will furthermore take our soul nature into the future in so far as it has learnt something, then we are looking at things the right way. But it must have learnt those things in a really living way. Even within this one incarnation, we can really confirm this. We can compare three people. The first person plunges straight into action. At a certain point in his life, he feels the urge to acquire self-knowledge. So he looks at the things he has always done well. He revels in what he has done well, and thus he decides to go on doing what he has always done well. In a certain sense, he is bound to do well, isn't he?

A second person is inclined to be more of a hypochondriac, and he looks more at his failings. If he can get over his hypochondria and his failings at all, he will get to the point of avoiding them. But he will not attain what a third could attain who says to himself, "What has happened was necessary, but at the same time, it is a basis for learning, learning through observation, not useless criticism." He will set to work in a living way, not perpetuating what has already happened and simply carrying the past into the future, but will strengthen and steel the companion part of himself and carry it livingly into the future. He will not merely repeat what he did well and avoid what he did badly, but by taking both the good and the bad into himself and simply letting it rest there, he will be strengthening and steeling it.

This is the very best way of fortifying the soul: to leave alone what has happened and carry it over livingly into the future. Otherwise we keep going back in a luciferic-ahrimanic way over past happenings. We can progress in our development only if we handle necessity properly. Why? Is there a right way of handling things in this area? In conclusion, I want to give you something like an illustration of this too, about which I want you to think a little between now and next Tuesday. Then, taking this illustration as our starting point, we shall be able to get a little further with our problem.

Suppose you want to see an external object. You can see it, though you cannot possibly do so if you place a mirror between the object and yourself. In that case you see your own eyes. If you want to see the object, you must renounce seeing your own eyes, and if you want to see your own eyes, you must renounce the sight of the object. Now, by a remarkable interworking of beings in the world, it is true with regard to human action and human knowledge that all our knowledge comes to us in a certain sense by way of a mirror. Knowing always means that we actually know in a certain sense by way of reflection.

So if we wish to look at our past actions, we actually always look at them by putting what is in fact a mirror between the actions and ourselves. But when we want to act, if we want to have a direct connection between ourselves and our action, between ourselves and the world, we must not put up the mirror. We must look away from what mirrors ourselves. This is how it is with regard to our past actions. The moment we look at them, we place a mirror in front of them, and then we can certainly have knowledge of them. We can leave the mirror there and know them in every terrible detail. There will certainly be cases where this will be a very good thing. But if we are not capable of taking the mirror away again, then none of our knowledge will be any good to us. The moment we take the mirror away we no longer see ourselves and our past actions, but it is only then that they can enter into us and become one with us.

This is how we should proceed with self-observation. We must realize that as long as we look back, this review can only be the inducement for us to take what we have seen into us livingly. But we must not keep on looking at it, otherwise the mirror will always be there. Self-observation is very similar to looking at ourselves in a mirror. We can make progress in life only if we take what we learn through self-observation into our will as well.

Please take this illustration to heart, the illustration of seeing one's own eyes only if one renounces seeing something else, and of the fact that if one wants to see something else, one must renounce seeing one's own eyes. Take this illustration to heart. Then, taking this illustration as a basis, let us talk next Tuesday about right and wrong self-observation, and get nearer and nearer to the solution of our problems. In this most difficult of human problems, the problem of freedom and necessity and the interrelationship of human action and world events, it is certainly necessary that we face all the difficulties. And those who believe they can solve this problem before they have dealt with all the difficulties in fact are mistaken.

The MIRROR is the MAPs we made of our past experience

Lecture IV

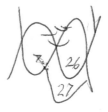

February 1, 1916

We are far too accustomed to dealing with big problems like necessity and freedom in the simplest possible concepts and trying, as it were, in the twinkling of an eye to cover as many aspects as we can. We usually do not consider that problems of this kind require that we realize how complicated many of the interrelationships are in the world, and that what takes place in one area must be looked at in an entirely different light, if we want to understand it, than something quite similar in another area of the world.

I would like first of all to remind you of something I mentioned here a short time ago in a different connection. When we see such significant world events as those of the present, we are very much inclined to look hastily for the most obvious causes and to expect to find the consequences in what will happen immediately afterwards. With this kind of observation we do the facts a thorough injustice. When I mentioned this before, I drew your attention to the fact that at the beginning of the Middle Ages the Roman world and what is now Central Europe were in opposition to one another. From a historical point of view we can say lightly, "Well, we try to discover the particular political motives of ancient Rome that made those Romans feel compelled to carry out their campaigns against the countries to their north, against what is now Central Europe. And we can look for the consequences in subsequent developments."

Yet if we look at things this way we do not by any

means exhaust all the points that should be considered. For just imagine, if something different had happened in the way the tribes moved across Europe from east to west, or something had happened differently in the clash between the might of Rome and the Teutonic tribes, the whole subsequent development of Central Europe right up to modern times would have had a different appearance. All the various events we have seen taking place in the course of the centuries up to our time would have been different if, at that time, the world of the ancient Roman people, who owing to their particular quality and their position in world history could not fully take up Christianity, had not fused with the world of historically young peoples who had taken up Christianity with youthful energy.

Out of the way this encounter came about between a culturally overly mature people, such as the Romans were, and a historically young people, such as the Teutonic people were in those days, all the later events have developed right up to Goethe's *Faust* and all that nineteenth century culture has produced. Could things have happened the way they did if that encounter had not occurred? Here, we are looking at a stream permeated with a strict inner necessity moving through world events and spreading out over immense regions. How could anyone at that time possibly have even wanted to arrange his actions in keeping with what has happened on the physical plane through the centuries from then until now?

What is taking place today is in turn the starting point of universal configurations that will of course be connected with current happenings; yet, as far as events on the physical plane are concerned, these configurations will on the face of it look very dissimilar to what takes place compressed into a short time span. I only

want to mention this so that you become aware
there are deep reasons behind what I already 1
tioned in connection with these studies, namely, ших
we do not get far by brooding and speculating about
how things are connected in the world. Imagine a Roman or a Teuton of the third or fourth century speculating on the possible consequences of the battles taking
place in that time, and how far he would have got. Not
very far!

It is essential that we become aware that the deciding
factors concerning things that have to happen and our
recognition that they really ought to happen are not our
speculations about their possible results or immediate
consequences but other things. It is essential that we
become aware that into the stream of events taking
place on the physical plane there actually enter forces
we sense as coming from the spiritual world, impulses
about the particular effects of which we don't need to
speculate in regard to what ought to happen on the
physical plane. We must be in no doubt that looking at
human action and world history shows clearly how necessary it is that we should extend our view beyond what
lies on the physical plane. And after having prepared
the way for these essentials, let us return to considering
the human being as such.

In the last lecture I showed how impossible it is to
acquire a right relationship to our past actions if we
merely continue mulling them over. On the contrary,
we must realize that what is past, including our own
actions, belongs to the realm of necessity, and we must
become familiar with the thought that what happened
had to happen. That is to say, we acquire a right relationship to our actions if we can look objectively at our
past achievements, looking at a successful or unsuccessful deed of ours with equal objectivity.

Now you are bound to have serious objections to what I have just said, for such objections do exist. Consider for a moment what I have just said, that when we have done something, it is over; that we establish a proper attitude to it by facing it objectively and not wishing we had acted differently. The serious objection is this: What about the whole domain that should play a great part in human life, the domain of repentance for a deed we have done? Obviously people are quite right in saying that repentance is necessary and has to take place. If we could manage to remove from the human soul the feeling of regret, we would be removing a moral impulse of the highest order. But are we not actually doing away with it when we simply look at all that has happened completely objectively?

Here indeed is a new difficulty, one that can be the starting point for endless misunderstandings. We will have to go to the heart of the question of freedom if we want to clear away this difficulty. You know, the great Spinoza said that when we look at the world, we can really only speak of necessity.[1] Freedom is fundamentally a kind of illusion. For if a ball is hit by another one, it has to go the way the second one goes. "If it had consciousness it would believe"—so Spinoza says, and I mentioned this in my *Philosophy of Spiritual Activity*—that it was going its way by choice. And it is the same with the human being," says Spinoza.[2] "Even though he is in the clutches of necessity, just because he is conscious of what he does, he thinks he is free."

But Spinoza is utterly and totally wrong. The matter is quite different. If we really flew off somewhere like the ball that follows only the necessity of propulsion, we would lose consciousness regarding everything to do with our flying and our acting out of necessity. We would be bound to be unconscious of it. Consciousness

74

would be eliminated. And that is what happens. Just think of the speed with which you are moving through space according to the science of astronomy! You most certainly do not do that consciously. There, consciousness is cut out. You would not be capable of being conscious, for you would not be able to hurtle through space as the science of astronomy shows you do. Consciousness of everything a person does out of necessity has to be eliminated, and in such an obvious case as flying through space we can readily see that processes subject to necessity eliminate our consciousness.

However, we are not always so obviously conscious of things, but more or less unconscious of them. In real life it is very difficult to distinguish one from the other. Where one thing borders on another we cannot understand them as easily as in our case above. On the contrary, we could say, "In all matters where we are absolutely conscious, our actions cannot be other than free. If a ball that I struck really had consciousness, it would only fly in a certain direction if it received into its consciousness the impulse I gave it and directed its own course accordingly. The ball would first of all have to become unconscious in order merely to follow the momentum."

If you think this over, you will make a distinction that we unfortunately do not make in ordinary life with regard to actions. The fact that we do not make this distinction has not only a theoretical significance but also a very practical one. We do not in fact distinguish between situations where we have been unsuccessful and cases that are immoral and bad. This distinction is an extraordinarily important one. It is absolutely true that we arrive at a correct estimate of an action that has not succeeded and has not turned out as we intended only if we can look at it objectively as though it had been absolutely necessary. For as soon as it is over it is in the realm of absolute necessity. If something does not work out and we feel uncomfortable later on because it has not worked out, it is absolutely true that our uneasiness arises from egotism. One would have liked to have been a better person, a more capable person. That is egotism expressing itself. And unless this egotism is completely rooted out, we cannot see the further development of our soul in as significant a light as we should.

But not every deed we have done is an unsuccessful one; there can also be a bad deed, a morally bad deed. Let us look at morally bad deeds, for instance, the following one, to choose a really striking example. Suppose someone has nothing to eat, or would like something for some other reason than hunger, and he steals. Stealing is a bad deed, isn't it? Does what we have said keep a person who has stolen something from feeling remorse for his deed? No, it does not! And why not? For the very simple reason that he did not seriously want to steal, but only wanted to possess what he stole. He could readily have cut out the stealing if you had given him what he wanted, or if he had been able to acquire it in some other way than by stealing.

This is a striking case, but in a certain way it applies to all forms of bad deeds. The bad deed as such is never really intended, and language has a subtle feeling for this. When an evil deed has been done, we say, "conscience stirs." Why does conscience stir? Because the bad deed only now becomes a matter of knowledge. It comes up into consciousness. When the deed happened, the awareness was taken up by the motive on account of which the bad deed was done. A bad deed is not willed. And repenting means that the perpetrator becomes aware that he allowed his consciousness to be dulled at the time the bad deed was done. Whenever

76

anyone does a bad deed, it is always a matter of his consciousness of the deed being dulled, and of his having to acquire an awareness of cases like the one in which his consciousness was dimmed. The whole point of punishment is to awaken forces in the soul that will enable consciousness to extend to the kind of situations that previously produced an elimination of consciousness.

Among the dissertations done at universities by philosophers who are also occupied with legal problems there is usually one on "the right to administer punishment." Now a great many theories have been drawn up concerning reasons for giving punishment. The one and only possible reason can be found only when we realize that punishment is given for the sake of exerting the soul forces so that consciousness will extend into spheres it did not previously reach. This is also the task of repentance. Its purpose is precisely to let us observe the deed in such a way that the force of the repentance raises the action into consciousness. Then the consciousness will see the whole picture and will not be dulled the next time. You see what is involved. We must learn to discriminate properly between a fully conscious deed and one where the consciousness is dimmed.

On the other hand, if you have an action that does not fit the category of good or bad but was only unfortunate, an action in which something we had intended to do was not successful, there the point is that we ourselves can obscure our view of it if we judge it by bringing in the thought, the feeling, that it would perhaps have turned out differently if we had done this or that better, or if we ourselves had been different. Here, it is a matter of bearing in mind that if the eye is to see an object, it cannot see itself. It must hold up a mirror, for the moment the eye holds up a mirror to see itself, it cannot see the object. The moment a person broods about how differently he should have acted, the deed cannot act upon him with the kind of power that will further his soul development. For as soon as you set egotism between yourself and your deed, as implied in the fact that you would really like to have done the deed differently, you are doing exactly the same as when you hold a mirror in front of your eye so that it cannot see the object.

We can also put it another way. You know there are so-called astigmatic eyes, eyes in which the cornea are curved in different degrees in the perpendicular and the horizontal direction. Eyes like that have a peculiar kind of inaccurate vision. Such persons see specters merely because the cornea has an irregular curve. They see specters because they are actually perceiving their own eyes and not what is outside. If one perceives one's own eye because it is incorrectly constructed and has not become an eye that can completely eliminate itself and allow the object to affect it, one cannot perceive the object. If we fill our mind with the thought "You should have been different, and if you had only done this or that differently, it would all have turned out well," it is just as though we had astigmatism and did not see the actual fact but distorted it. Yet a person must see the real facts allotted him, only then will they really be effective. Their effect on a person who is not filled with feeling about facts but allows the facts themselves to work upon him will be the same as the effect an outside object has on healthy eyes. The facts then continue their work in the soul.

One can say that anyone who has not yet acquired an objective view of past facts in which he was involved cannot see them in their objectivity and therefore cannot obtain from them what he ought to have for his soul. It is exactly as though our eyes were to remain at their stage of development in the sixth or seventh month of embryonic growth, while we ourselves were born at the proper time. We would see the whole world wrongly. If the eyes were not to continue developing during the sixth, seventh, eighth, and ninth month, but were to stop short, they would not eliminate themselves in the process of seeing. We would see something entirely different from what we actually see when we develop normally.

Thus what we have done acquires its right value only when we have come to the point of being able to let it enter the stream of necessity, and when we can regard it as necessity. But as has been said, we must realize that we then have to make the distinction between what is successful and unsuccessful and what is called "good" or "bad" in a moral sense.

Broadly speaking, you will find all this analyzed, though more philosophically, in my *Philosophy of Spiritual Activity* for there it is emphasized that human beings become free when they achieve the possibility of drawing impulses from the spiritual world. In one passage it is even expressly stated that impulses of free will come from the spiritual world. However, that does not exclude the utmost freedom in relation to certain events in which we very distinctly follow necessity. For we must distinguish between purely external physical necessity and spiritual necessity, although the two are basically pretty much the same. But they differ in regard to the position they occupy in world existence.

It is like this: Let us look again at a figure such as Goethe, who has appeared in world history and of whom one can say that we can follow up the education of a person such as he, and can see how he became what he was; we can then follow up the impulse that led him to achieve his *Faust* and his other poetical works. We can, as it were, regard all that Goethe achieved as if it were the result of his education. And then of course we see him as a genius. We certainly can. By doing this we remain focused on Goethe.

But we can do it another way. We can follow the spiritual development in the eighteenth century. We can pick out some details, for instance, that before Goethe had thought of writing a *Faust*, Lessing had projected one, so there was already one in existence.[3] Thus we can say that the conception of *Faust* arose out of the spiritual problems and impulses of the time. We could say that if we examine Lessing's projected *Faust* and a number of other similar *Faust* versions, they all led to the famous *Faust*. By leaving Goethe out, we still come to *Faust* as though by necessity. *Faust* arose out of what preceded it. So we can arrive at *Faust* by following Goethe's development. One can look at Goethe from a more developmental point of view, or one can entirely leave him out and look in detail at how a type of poetry originated in Europe, such as the *Song of the Nibelungs*,[4] and how it became compressed into the poem *Parsifal*:[5] Parsifal, the striving human being, belonging to a certain period of evolution. One can look at how another line of development then came about, due to which the Parsifal concept was quite forgotten, and how that remarkable idea took hold of people that found its expression in the popular romance of *Faust*. This brought the appearance of a Faust about, what one might call a Parsifal of a later age. Goethe can be left out entirely.

Obviously we must not be pedantic; fifty years more or less do not matter. Time is elastic and can be stretched forward or backward, so that that does not interfere. It is only with things that go on in an ahrimanic way that time plays an important part. Things that come from the gods can always be moved forward or backward in time. But speaking generally we can say that even if the Frankfurt councillor Kaspar Goethe and his wife Aja had not had their son Wolfgang, or if he had died immediately after birth, for as you know he was ill at birth and nearly died, someone else would certainly have produced something similar to *Faust*. Similarly if Goethe had lived in the fourteenth century, he would certainly not have written *Faust*. These are unreal thoughts of course, but sometimes one has to consider them in order to realize the truth.

Thus we can now ask the question, "Did Goethe produce his *Faust* or any of his life's work out of freedom, or was it a question of absolute necessity?" The greatest freedom of all is to obey historical necessity! For if anyone imagines that his freedom could ever be endangered by what exists in the world as necessity, he ought also to say, "I want to create a poem, but I am a person who wants to work in total freedom! I want to disregard all the other poets who were unfree; I want to write a free poem. But I could not be free if I were to use the words of our language, for they came about through primeval necessity. That would not do! I will be an absolute champion of freedom. I will make up my own language!" And he sets about doing so. What he would actually achieve, of course, would be that everybody rejects him and his poem written in a nonexistent language, that with his freedom he would be bound to arouse everyone's resistance, which would express itself at first of course merely in incomprehension. From this you will see that there can be no talk of freedom, as it enters into the stream of events, being in any way encroached upon by the necessity present in the ongoing stream of world events.

We might also imagine a painter who wanted to be completely free saying, "I want to paint for sure, but I do not want to paint on a canvas or any other surface; I will paint freely. Do I first of all experiment on a given material? Not me! For then I would perpetually be compelled to comply with its surface." The material has a very definite conformity to law, yet complying with it does not mean one is not free.

Particularly where major events in world history are concerned, it is obvious that when consciousness plays a part in our actions, what we can call necessity can join directly with freedom. As I have already said, in the fourteenth century Goethe would not have been able to create *Faust*, for it would have been absolutely impossible for *Faust* to have come about at that time. He would not have been able to write it. Why not? Because there is something we have to call an empty space in world events with regard to certain evolutionary impulses. Just as we cannot put more water into a cask if it is already full, or we can only put a certain quantity into it if it is already partly full, we cannot put anything we please into an already "full" age.

In the fourteenth century there was no space for anything like the kind of thing that came down from the spiritual world through a human being into the physical world in the form of *Faust*; no space, only a state of fullness. Events run their course in cycles, and when a cycle has been completed, an empty space appears for new impulses which can then enter the life of the world. A cycle has to be complete in regard to content, and then an empty space must occur again, before new impulses can come in. In the cultural period in which Goethe lived, an empty space had occurred for the impulses that came from the spiritual world to the physical world through him. Evolution really does proceed in

[handwritten marginalia: Ages are like casks — if we can't add anything to a full one]

waves: emptiness—a state of fullness to the point of completion—an ebbing—emptiness again. Then something new can come.

In the time between death and a new birth a human being plans his next incarnation according to this rhythm. He arranges it so that he encounters the particular level of emptiness or fullness in the physical world that is right for his impulses. Someone bringing with him from earlier incarnations impulses of the highest order that require a space must come at a time when there is an empty space. Whoever has the kind of impulses that need to meet with receptivity must incarnate at a time when there is a space to be filled. In many areas of course one thing will work in opposition to another. That is quite obvious. We see then that in a certain respect we choose—if we may use the word—on the strength of our inner qualities the period in which we come into the world. And on this depends the inner necessity governing our activities.

If you bear this in mind, you will no longer see any contradiction in the consecutive events and realize that Parsifal and so on, and Faust, take their turns, and then comes Goethe who creates a work that can just as well be understood in the succession of periods. You will find no contradiction any longer, because Goethe looked down from above and prepared in his inner being what could become tangible in his work. That is to say, when he was on the physical plane, he brought forth from his inner being what he had absorbed in those particular preceding centuries in which the stream of events had taken place.

Between the two statements "Goethe's work had to be produced at a definite time," and "Goethe produced it out of freedom" there is just as little contradiction as there would be if I were to have a board and six balls in a row, then produce a small cup and say, "I will put the first ball into the cup, then the second and third and so on, and I pour them out over here." And if now someone were to say, "But those balls lying over there are the same balls we had to start with," someone else could reply, "No, they are the balls that came out of the cup." Both statements can be true.

What took place in the course of time and ultimately led to *Faust* is what Goethe had absorbed in his inner being and what Goethe then expressed just because it had accumulated within him through looking down from the spiritual world. For we always take part in the whole evolution of the world. If we look at things this way, we can say "The moment we look into the past we have to regard past events themselves as a necessity. And if we look at ourselves and produce the past again as deeds of the present, so long as we do this consciously, we are still free in what we bring into the present of what was prepared in the past out of necessity." Thus that person is most free of all who knows in full consciousness "what I am doing is nothing but spiritual necessity." These things cannot be understood by pedantic logic but only by fully grasping reality in a living way.

There is still another approach that can help us understand this completely. We can ask ourselves the following. If we look at animals, we know they have a dimmed consciousness. I have often described that. Human beings have a level of consciousness in which freedom can come to expression. But what kind of consciousness do angels have, the beings immediately above human beings? What is the consciousness of the angels like?

It is actually very difficult to have an immediate perception of the consciousness of angels. When we as

84

human beings want to do something, we consider what form our action is going to take. And if it does not work out on the physical plane as we imagined it should, we have failed. If someone sews two pieces of cloth together, and when he has finished it they come apart, the endeavor has not been a success. This can happen with a sewing machine. If things do not turn out as we had envisioned they would on the physical plane, we say the deed has miscarried. That is to say, people aim their will at something they picture happening on the physical plane. This is how our human willing proceeds.

But not in the case of angels. Their intention is everything. An angel's intention can be carried out in many different ways and the effect can still be exactly the same. This is quite true, though it is of course contrary to ordinary logic. In the artistic sphere only, and then only from the human point of view, can we acquire any feeling for this kind of consciousness. For you will always find that if the artist can take things in a human way—he may not always be in a position to do so, but if he can—he may possibly appreciate what turns out contrary to his expectations, even to the point of failure, and regard it to be of greater value than those things he did exactly as they should have been done. We then come a little closer to what is so extraordinarily difficult to grasp: that with the angels' consciousness, their will, everything depends on the intentions, and that these intentions may be realized in the most varied ways on the physical plane, even in polar opposite ways. That is to say, when an angel decides to do something, he chooses something quite definite, but not in the way that he says, "It has to look like this." That is not in the least implied. He will not know what it looks like until it has happened.

85

We have seen, and I have drawn your attention to the fact, that this is even the case with the Elohim. The Elohim created light and saw that it was good. This means that what comes first for human beings, the mental image of what is on the physical plane, does not come first at all in the consciousness of spiritual beings above human beings. With them the intention comes first, and how it is to be carried out is quite another matter. Now in this respect humans are of course mid-way between animals and angels. Therefore, they tend on the one hand to descend to the unconsciousness of animals. Whenever a criminal deed occurs, it is essentially due to the animality in human beings. On the other hand, however, we also have a tendency to ascend to the consciousness of the Angeloi. We have within us the possibility of developing a higher consciousness, a consciousness beyond the ordinary one, in which intentions take on a different aspect than is normally the case.

Thus we can say, that if as human beings we get involved in some of life's important problems, we cannot then make plans in the ordinary way. Suppose that as a teacher—a proper teacher this time—you have a particular child to educate. Now an average person has his educational principles. He knows when to give punishment and when not to; perhaps that he should never give any punishment at all. He knows how to do that. But if you look at the matter from the point of view of a higher consciousness, you will not always judge in this way, but will leave everything in life's hands. You will wait for the results of observation. Your one intention will be to bring out all the latent talents. But these potential talents can be drawn out in various ways. This is the important thing.

If we take all these things into consideration, we will

realize that in order to understand how necessity and freedom affect the human being we must observe both the external physical part and the inner part, first of all the etheric. I have already drawn your attention to the fact that our etheric body takes quite a different course from the physical body. Our physical body, as I once told you, is young to begin with. It then develops and grows older until it becomes senile. The etheric body does the opposite. Whereas we say we grow older when speaking of the physical body, we ought really to say we grow younger as regards the etheric body. If we want to use the words "old" and "young" for the etheric body, it is actually old when we are born, for it is all wrinkled up and small enough to fit us. When we reach a normal old age, and die, our etheric body has become so rejuvenated that we can hand it over to the whole world, where it can work again as a youthful force. While the physical grows older, the etheric body grows younger. It gets younger and younger.

If we die at an unusual time, die young, significant things can happen with the etheric body, such as those I have told you about. But it is not only with regard to aging that we see a difference between the physical and etheric bodies, but also with regard to necessity and freedom. When the human being is most enmeshed in necessity in what he does with the physical body or in general as a being on the physical plane, he is then freest in his etheric body, and the latter is then left entirely to itself. Whenever the etheric body is enmeshed in necessity, everything a person does on the physical plane is left to his own freedom. Thus, where the physical body is subject to necessity, the etheric body has a corresponding degree of freedom, and where the etheric body is subject to necessity, the physical body has a certain amount of freedom.

Let us look at what this means. You cannot say we are completely free to get up and go to bed whenever we want to. People get up in the morning and go to bed in the evening. There is no question of freedom there. This is part of the iron necessities of life. And even if you vary the time of getting up and going to bed, freedom is obviously out of the question. You also eat every day. There is no question of freedom there. You cannot resolve to do away with this necessity and try to be free by not eating, because you feel the taking in of food to be a compulsion. With regard to all these things a human being is tied to necessity. And why is he tied to necessity? Because the companion—as I called him last time—the inner self accompanying us through life on the physical plane and through all the compulsions connected with the physical plane, lives all the while in freedom.

But if we are to involve our inner being, our etheric body, in necessity, how are we to do it? By consciously submitting to what we recognize to be a necessity. For instance, by telling ourselves that the time has come when everyone who realizes he is ready for spiritual science ought to take it up. Nobody is forced to do this by an external necessity, of course. But we can see it as an inner necessity, because it is necessary in the present cycle of humanity. Thus out of our own free will we yield to necessity. There is no external pressure on the physical plane. We must follow compulsion out of inner freedom, as it were. The etheric body itself makes the resolve, which permeates it with necessity; it creates the necessity itself, thus acquiring the possibility of developing in freedom with regard to what happens on the physical plane. That is to say, we become acquainted with spiritual necessity, thereby making ourselves more and more free with regard to life on the physical plane.

88

You will now say, "Through the very fact that we find our way into a spiritual necessity we ought to become more and more free in life on the physical plane." That is indeed so. By uniting ourselves with the spirit that streams through the world and letting it pass through us, we really do receive elements that set us free from the fetters of the physical world. We cannot of course free ourselves from what is allotted us by our previous incarnation, by our karma. But if we do not thus free ourselves through our knowledge of spiritual necessity from conditions of necessity on the physical plane, we remain bound to these after death, and have to carry them with us. We have to carry the necessities of the physical plane with us through the life between death and a new birth, and cannot free ourselves from them. But each moment in which we connect ourselves in our etheric body with the necessities of the spiritual plane, we become freer and freer of the necessities of the physical plane.

It is indeed so that if we can follow out of a free resolve a purely spiritual impulse, we become freer and freer from all that would otherwise fetter us to physical life, fetter us far beyond death. On the other hand, with regard to everything we are enmeshed in during physical life, and which is unalterable, the etheric body as such becomes freer and freer.

Thus we see how freedom and necessity interact on the physical plane and also in connection with the etheric body. The etheric body receives its freedom through the necessity of the physical plane, and has to recognize its own necessity. The physical body receives its freedom when the etheric body thus recognizes its necessity, and its necessity arises through its self-chosen karmic involvement in the events on the physical plane.

In this way we see the physical part of human beings, free in bondage, and the spiritual-soul part, bound in freedom, interacting organically. Freedom and necessity always interweave. It is quite impossible for us to be subject to pure necessity when we are fully conscious. Through the fact that we permeate a thing with consciousness, that is to say, accept it in full consciousness, freedom governs our soul. This is how we lift ourselves out of necessity in our soul and make ourselves free concerning matters we are conscious of. However, if we acknowledge with our minds that something is necessary, for instance, that the present time is the time for taking part in spiritual science, if we freely comply with a necessity, so to speak, does this give us a degree of unconsciousness? In a certain sense it does. We do become unconscious to the extent that we undertake to develop our consciousness to the point where we reach the gate through which streams and radiates what is to come from the spiritual world. We then receive this, and bend to the powerful forces coming to meet us from the spirit world. This is why in connection with working our way into spiritual necessity we speak of working our way up to the beings who bend down toward us.

Therefore we shall always stress that with our consciousness we soar toward the beings who permeate and pulse through us from the spiritual world and when we say, "We must of necessity accommodate ourselves to the impulses coming from the spiritual world," we expect that at the same time the impulses of higher spiritual beings will descend into these our impulses. Thus a relative, deep unconsciousness arises, where we become aware of what is at work in us spiritually in the same way as we would be aware of an unconscious action where we are quite sure that the spirit is in us

90

and the right thing to do is to obey, where we are privileged to obey.

We have now come back to our starting point. If we tried with our ordinary consciousness to mull over the many consequences that can arise from such significant events as those of the present, for instance—and I compared them earlier to the Roman-Teutonic wars—we would get nowhere. However, the moment we can tell ourselves we do not want to find the right solution through mulling them over but through giving way to the spiritual impulse and letting it stream in, we do not need to brood. For then we know that if only we let these spiritual impulses take hold of us, they lead us to the right solution, to spiritual currents that even go beyond the centuries, beyond millennia. This is what is important.

Then we see that we no longer need to think that things must go like this today and like that tomorrow for such and such to happen, for we will realize that we are now living in the particular epoch of humanity in which the further evolution of earthly existence can progress in the right way only if spiritual impulses coming from the spiritual world are directly taken up. That is how it is. And the things that happen externally on the physical plane must of necessity unite with these impulses in the right way. Then the right things will happen. Then we shall know, without mulling over what will happen tomorrow and the day after tomorrow, that what will really come about will be that the souls now passing through the gate of death will continue to work on, both in their etheric bodies and as souls, to the extent that the thoughts of those human beings who will in the future populate the blood-stained battlefields of the earth join with them, so that something will arise that will live for centuries. But we must have a direct awareness of this in the spirit of these words we have often heard:

> Out of the courage of the fighters,
> Out of the blood of battles,
> Out of the grief of the bereaved,
> Out of the peoples' deeds of sacrifice
> There shall arise spirit fruit
> If only souls, in spirit-mindfulness,
> Will reach out to the spirits' realm.

The important thing to realize is that from a certain point in the present on souls must become conscious of the spirit, souls that have the will to direct their consciousness toward the spirit. Then, from what is happening today, the right things will come for the future. To make this thought our own, steadfast confidence is needed, such as those beings have whom we count as members of the hierarchy of the angels. For angels act out of that kind of confidence. They know that if they have the right intentions, the right things will come of them; not because they envision that future events should take a definite form, but because they have the right intentions. These right intentions, however, can only be grasped spiritually. And only through thinking in the way of spiritual science can we find the way to grasp something spiritually, as we have endeavored to do.

92

Lecture V

February 8, 1919

I have a few things to add to the four lectures on freedom and necessity which more or less form a connected whole. Let us take another look at one of our basic truths of spiritual science, the structure of the human being that we have become so well acquainted with. We consider man as a synthesis of four members: the physical body, the etheric body, the astral body and the *I*. If we confine ourselves to what is in the physical world, to the part of the human being that is given, we can state that in our ordinary waking condition we have in the first place the physical body. We know our physical body for the very reason that we can obviously observe it externally with our senses, and everyone else in the physical world can observe it in the same way and has to agree with us that the physical body exists. Therefore, in the physical world this physical body can be perceived from outside.

A simple reflection can convince you that you cannot observe what we usually call the etheric body. It escapes ordinary physical observation. The astral body also escapes ordinary physical observation, and the *I* even more so, for the essence of the *I*, as we have often said, can be so little observed externally that human beings cannot even name it from outside. If someone were to call out the word "I" to you, you would never come to the conclusion that he could mean your *I*. He can only mean his own *I*. The *I* as such is never named from outside. Yet it is obvious that we know something about

Those things which we cannot name from the outside we are unconscious of it, up until now.

it. We name it from within. Thus we can say after all that while the etheric and the astral body are inaccessible on the physical plane, as things stand now, the *I* is not inaccessible. We refer to it by saying "I." Nevertheless, it remains a fact that the *I* cannot be seen in the same way as the physical body or any other physical object. It cannot be perceived at all by the senses.

What does the fact that we know something about the *I* and that we come to the point of naming it actually tell us about the *I*? Philosophers often say, "Human beings have direct certainty of the *I*. They know firsthand that the *I* exists." In fact, there are philosophers who imagine they know merely from philosophy that the *I* is a primary being, that it cannot be dispersed or die. Yet anyone with sound thinking will immediately respond to this philosophical opinion by saying, "However much you prove to us that the *I* cannot be dissolved and therefore cannot fade away, it is quite enough that after death, probably for eternity, the *I* is to be in the same condition it is in between falling asleep and waking up." Then of course we would no longer be able to speak of an *I*. Philosophers are mistaken if they imagine there is any reality in the *I* they speak of. If we speak of something that really exists, we are speaking of something entirely different.

Between falling asleep and awakening the *I* is not there, and a person cannot say "I" to himself. If he dreams about his *I*, it sometimes even strikes him as though he is encountering a picture of himself, that is to say, he looks at himself. He does not call himself "I" as he does in ordinary daily life. When we wake up, it is in regard to our true *I* as though we were to strike against the resistance of our physical body. We know, don't we, that the process of waking up consists of our *I* coming into our physical body. (Our astral body also does so, but for the moment we are interested in the *I*.) The experience of coming in feels like hitting our hand against a solid object, and the counterthrust, so to speak, that this experience engenders is what brings about our consciousness of our *I*. And throughout our waking day we are not really in possession of our *I*, for what we have is a mental image of our *I* reflected back from our physical body. Thus what we normally know of the *I* from philosophy is a reflection, a mirror image of the *I*. Do we have nothing more than this ego reflection? Well, this reflection obviously ceases when we go to sleep. The *I* is no longer reflected. Thus on falling asleep our *I* would really disappear. Yet in the morning when we wake up, it enters our physical body again. So it must have continued to exist.

What can this *I* be, then? How much of it do we possess so long as we are active solely on the physical plane? If we investigate further, we have, to begin with, nothing of this *I* within the physical world except will, acts of will. All we can do is will. The fact that we are able to will makes us aware of being an *I*. Sleep happens to be a dimming of our will; for reasons we have often discussed we cannot exert our will during sleep. The will is then dimmed. We do not will during sleep. Thus what is expressed in the word *I* is a true act of will, and the mental picture we have of the *I* is a reflection that arises when our will impinges on our body. This impact is just like looking into the mirror and seeing our physical body. Thus we see our own *I* as an expression of will through its effect on the body. This gives us our mental image of the *I*. Therefore, on the physical plane the *I* lives as an act of will.

So we already have a duality on the physical plane: our physical body and our *I*. We know of our physical body because we can picture it with our observation outside in space; and we know of our *I* through the fact that we can will. Everything else underlying the physical body cannot at first be discovered through physical observation. We can see how the physical body has developed and what it is composed of. Yet the description we have to give of this composition in the course of our passage through the Saturn, sun, moon, and earth evolutions remains a mystery if we consider the physical body only. Everything underlying the physical body is a mystery to physical observation in the physical world.

How the will enters our physical body, or enters into what we are, is a further mystery. For you can become conscious of your will, can't you. Therefore, Schopenhauer[1] regarded the will as the only reality, because he had an inkling that in the will we actually become conscious of ourselves. But of how this will enters into us we know nothing at all on the physical plane. On the basis of the physical world, we know only that in our *I* we can take hold of our will. I pick up this watch, but how this act of will passes through the etheric body into the physical body and actually turns into a picking up of the watch remains a mystery even for the physical body. The will descends straight from the *I* into the physical body. Nothing else remains in the *I* but the inner feeling, the inner experience of the will.

The way I have described this here has actually been applicable to the greater part of humanity only for the past few centuries, and this fact is usually overlooked. As for us, we have studied the matter so much that it ought to have become second nature with us. If we look back to the middle of medieval times, it is pure fancy to imagine that people lived then in exactly the same way as they do today. Humanity evolves, and the way human beings relate to the world changes in the different epochs.

If we go back beyond the fifteenth and fourteenth centuries, we find many more people than we do now who not only knew of the physical body but who really knew that something lived in the physical body that we nowadays call the etheric body, people who actually perceived something of the aura of the physical body. By the Middle Ages of course these were only the last remnants of an ancient perception. Even in the tenth century, though, people did not look into a person's eyes like we do today when we simply see the physical eyes. When they looked at other people's eyes, they still saw something of the aura, the etheric. They had a way of seeing uprightness or falsehood in the eyes, not through any kind of external judgment but through direct perception of the aura around the eyes. It was also like this with other things.

In addition to perceiving the aura of human beings, people then saw it to a far greater extent than now in animals and also in plants. You all know the description in my book *Knowledge of the Higher Worlds* that if we observe one seed, we see it shining differently from other grains of seed.[2] Nowadays this perception can only be achieved through training, but in earlier centuries it was still quite an ordinary, everyday phenomenon. People did not first have to investigate, possibly with a microscope, what plant a seed came from—even that can in many cases no longer be done today—for they were able to determine such things from the light aura surrounding the seed. And in the case of minerals too, you will find descriptions in old writings classifying them in a certain way according to their value in the world. When the ancients looked at gold, what they described was not invention, for to them gold really appeared in a different way from silver, for instance. When they connected gold with sunlight and silver with moonlight, this was really founded on observation. When they said, "Gold is pure sunlight that has been condensed, silver is moonlight," and so on, they expressed what they saw in the same way as they still saw elemental life in the outside world, the elemental aura that modern people have lost sight of because modern mankind has to evolve to freedom, which can only be acquired by a complete restriction of observation to what is physically objective.

Just as human beings have lost the ability to see these auras, they have also lost another ability. Today, we must acquire a feeling for how very different it was when the ancients spoke of the will. They had much more of a feeling of how the will, which nowadays lives only in the *I*, entered the organic realm, the astral body as we would say today. They still felt the *I* continuing on into the astral body. This can be explained in a quite specific field.

The fact that painters believe they can no longer manage without a model is due to their having totally lost the faculty of experiencing in any way at all how the *I* continues on into the organism, into the astral body. Why is it often precisely the old portraits that people admire today? Because they were not painted as they now are, where the artist merely has a sitter to copy, and is duty bound to copy everything that is there. In the past people knew that if a person forms the muscles round his eyes in a particular way, then what lives in his *I* enters in a very definite way into his astral body and produces this form of the muscles. If we were to go back as far as ancient Greece, we would be quite wrong to imagine that the ancient Greeks used a model for the wonderful forms they created. They had no models. If a particular curve of the arm was required, the sculptor, knowing how the will brought the *I* into the astral body, created the curve out of this experience. As this feeling for what was going on in the astral body faded away the necessity arose to adhere as strictly to a model as is customary today.

The essential difference is that in fairly recent times human beings have come to the point where they see the outer world devoid of all its aura and see themselves inwardly with no awareness of the fact that the will ripples into the astral body and throughout the whole organism. Things have only been like this for a short while.

After a much longer time has elapsed, a new age will arrive for humanity. Then even more will have been taken away from both the outer aspect of the physical plane and from man's inner awareness. We know that at present we are only a few centuries into the fifth post-Atlantean epoch that began in the fourteenth century, for we count the fourth post-Atlantean epoch from approximately the founding of Rome till the fifteenth century, and the fifth post-Atlantean epoch from the fifteenth century till as long again; so we are now only in the first third of it. But mankind is steering toward an entirely different kind of perception. We are moving toward a time when the outer world will be far more bleak and empty. Nowadays when a person looks at nature, he believes it to be green and the vault of heaven to be blue. He sees nature in such a way that he believes the colors to be the outcome of a natural process.

In the sixth post-Atlantean epoch he will no longer be able to believe in the colors of nature. At present the physicists only talk about there being nothing outside

99

us but vibrations, and that it is these that, for example, bring about red in us. What the physicists dream of today will come true. At present they only dream of it, but it will then be true. People will no longer be able to distinguish properly between a red face and a pale one. They will know that all those things are caused by their own organism. They will consider it a superstition that there are colors outside that tint objects. The outer world will be grey in grey and human beings will be conscious of the fact that they themselves put the colors into the world. Just as people today say, "Oh, you crazy anthroposophers, you talk about there being an etheric body, but it is not true, you only dream it into people!" People who then see only the outer reality will say to the others who still see colors in their full freshness, "Oh, you dreamers! Do you really believe there are colors outside in nature? You do not know that you are only dreaming inside yourself that nature has these colors." Outer nature will become more and more a matter of mathematics and geometry. Just as today we can do no more than speak of the etheric body, and people in the world outside do not believe that it exists, people in the future will not believe that the capacity to see colors in the outer world has any objective significance; they will ascribe it purely to subjectivity.

Humanity will have a similar experience in regard to the relationship of the will in their *I* to the outer world. They will reach the point where they will have only the very slightest awareness of the impulses that come to expression in their will. They will have scarcely any awareness of the unique personal experience of willing anything out of the *I*. What is willed out of the *I* will only have a very faint effect on a person. If all that mankind receives by nature continues along the lines described, then in order to do anything at all people will need either long practice or outer compulsion. People will not get up of their own accord, but will have to learn it until it becomes a habit. The mere resolve to get up will not make the slightest impression. This would be an abnormal condition at present, but natural evolution as such is tending in this direction. People will have less belief in moral ideals. Outer dictates will be necessary to activate the will.

This would be the natural course of events, and those who know that what comes later is prepared beforehand know that the sixth epoch is being prepared in the fifth. After all, you can see with half an eye that a large part of humanity is tending in this direction. People are aiming more and more at having everything drummed into them, at being spoonfed, and consider it the right procedure to be told what to do. As I said, we are now roughly in the first third of the fifth post-Atlantean epoch, i.e., in an age in which—although the physicists already have the ideal of the sixth age—there is still the belief that colors really do exist outside, and that it is a human attribute to have a red or a pale face. Nowadays we still believe this. We can of course allow ourselves to be persuaded by the physicists or physiologists that we imagine colors, but we do not really believe it. We believe that the nature we live in on the physical plane has its own colors.

We are in the first third of the fifth post-Atlantean epoch, which will obviously have three thirds. During these three thirds post-Atlantean humanity has to pass through various experiences, the first one being that people have to become fully conscious of what I have just described. People must realize fully that in their considerations of the physical body they have completely lost sight of what is behind the physical, totally lost sight of it in all respects. In the second third of the fifth post-Atlantean epoch—if spiritual science has been successful—there will be more and more people who will know with certainty that something more, something of an etheric-spiritual nature, is bound up with what we see around us. People will begin to be conscious of the fact that what existed in earlier times for clairvoyance, and is now no longer a part of our relation to the world, must be rediscovered in a different way. We will not be able to rediscover the aura that used to be seen, but if people accept and practice exercises, such as those given in *Knowledge of the Higher Worlds*, they will realize that they can rediscover along a different path that an auric element surrounds and interpenetrates the human being and everything else in the world. People will acquire a consciousness of this once again.

People will also become aware that they are able to grasp moral impulses once again. However, they will have to take hold of them with a stronger resolve than they do today, for there is a natural tendency in the will to gradually lose its impelling power. The will must be taken hold of more firmly. This kind of will can be developed if people are determined to exercise the strong thinking necessary for the understanding of the truths of spiritual science. People who do understand these truths will be pouring more strength into their will, and they will therefore acquire, instead of a will that is deteriorating to the point of paralysis, a powerful will, able to act freely out of the *I*.

As humanity progresses, merely natural development will be counteracted by the efforts people make: on the one hand, efforts to do the exercises of spiritual science in order to become aware once more of the aura, and on the other hand, efforts to strengthen themselves by means of the impulses coming from spiritual science for the invigorating and activating of the will.

It is actually as follows. What has to be developed by spiritual science in the second third of the fifth post-Atlantean epoch does not yet exist at all. What is the position of human beings today when they observe the external world? And how do scientists stand in this regard? It is very instructive to look at the position of present-day science, especially present-day scientists—of course only in so far as this science presents the natural relation of human beings to their environment. When they look at outer, physical nature, whether it is the mineral, plant, animal, or human kingdom, neither modern scientists nor ordinary human beings have the power really to enter into what they observe. Physicists carry out experiments and then describe them. But they do not venture to fathom the mysteries of what they are describing. They do not feel able to search more deeply into the processes the experiments reveal. They remain on the surface. In relation to the outer world they are in exactly the same situation as you are when you are on a different plane when dreaming. You dream because your etheric body radiates the experiences of the astral body back to you. Anyone observing nature or making an experiment nowadays also observes what it radiates back to him, what it presents to him. He only dreams of nature. The moment he were to approach nature as spiritual science does, he would wake up. But he does not want to. In this first third of the fifth post-Atlantean epoch people only dream of nature. Human beings must wake up! Occasionally someone does wake up out of his dream, and says, "What is out there is no mere dream; there is something living within it."

Schopenhauer's philosophy was an awakening of this

kind, but he did not know what to do with it. It gave offense to those who philosophized cleverly in the modern way such as the eminent philosopher Bolzano of Bohemia did in the first half of the nineteenth century.[3] If you see his copy of Schopenhauer, you will find that he wrote in the margin, "Sheer madness!" Of course, it struck him as sheer madness, because the following statement was really made out of a kind of delirium, "There is something resembling will in outer nature."

And when modern science remains true to itself and, as it were, draws its own conclusions, what will it arrive at? Dreaming about the physical body! It has no inkling that there is something besides the physical body, otherwise it would have to speak of an etheric body, an astral body, and an *I*. It does not want to grasp reality, however, but only what presents itself. The modern physicist or physiologist feels like a somnambulist. He is dreaming and if someone shouts at him, which happens if someone talks to him about spiritual science, he falls down just like a somnambulist who is shouted at. And the impression he has is, "I am now in a void!" He cannot change immediately and has to go on dreaming. Just when he thinks he is most awake in relation to external nature he is dreaming most of all.

What will be the outcome? The modern physicist or physiologist will gradually lose all possibility of finding anything in the outer world except for his mental images of it. He will even gradually lose the capacity to form any idea of anything beyond his own mental images of the outer world. What is left for him if he relinquishes the human body to the scientist? The human body is there in front of him and he observes it in great detail, but he leaves it to the scientist or the medical profession to tell him what changes take place if one or another part does not function normally. He dissects this physical body very carefully. But he stops at that and has no notion that there is anything beyond it. In *this* physical body there is no trace of an *I* or of will.

What would this scientist actually have to do? He would have to deny the *I* and the will altogether and say, "There is no will, no trace of it exists in the human being, for we cannot find it." Down in the organism is where the will is hidden, imperceptibly. As we have said, it is only taken hold of, felt, and experienced in the *I*. Thus, the will would have to be shown in order to prove the existence of the *I*. That is to say, if a scientist who is only dreaming now were to be absolutely honest, we would hear him say to his audience, "When we speak of the human being, we ought really to speak of will. To us scientists that is an impossibility. The will is nothing. It is an absolutely unfounded hypothesis. It does not exist." That is what he ought to say if he were to be quite consistent. He would dream of external processes and deny the will.

I have not merely invented what I have just told you. It is an inevitable conclusion of the modern scientific view. If a scientist were to follow his way of thinking to its logical conclusion, he would arrive at what I have just told you. It is not mere invention on my part. I have brought along as an example the *Introduction to Physiological Psychology in Fifteen Lectures* written by the celebrated Professor Dr. Ziehen of Jena.[4] He endeavors here to describe what is manifest in the human being as a creature of body and soul. In the course of these lectures, he speaks about all the aspects of the sensations of smell, taste, hearing, sight, and so on. I will not bother you with all that, but will just discuss a few passages in the fifteenth lecture about the will. There you will find statements such as the following:

From the countless material stimuli of the outer world
we isolated stimuli of the cortex which correspond in the
psychological realm to sensations. We then followed
these sensations to the brain cortex along the associative
fibers into the motor zone from where the material
stimulus was led once again towards the muscular sys-
tem at the periphery where it caused muscular contrac-
tion. This transcortical process corresponded on a soul
level to the association of ideas, and the resultant movement we designate psychologically as action. We were
able to derive the latter sufficiently satisfactorily from
the sensation and from the memory pictures of previous
sensations, mental images functioning according to the
laws of the association of ideas, to be able to pursue the
psychic process to its final stage. At this point, however,
we encounter a hypothesis that used to be almost uni-
versally taught by psychology and which the ordinary
human understanding has always arrived at apparently
unconsciously. I refer to the assumption of a distinct
will as the cause of our actions.

Ziehen goes on to show that there is no sense in
speaking of such a will, that physiologists do not find
anything in any way corresponding to this word "will."
He also shows in the particular way he interprets the
effects of forces that one might call depravity of will,
that there too, it is not a matter of will but of something
quite different, so that we cannot speak of will at all.
    You see how consistent this is. If people get no fur-
ther than dreaming of the external physical world, they
cannot arrive at the will. They cannot find it at all. All
they can do if they create a world view, is to deny the
will as such and say, "So there cannot be a will." The
so-called monists of our time do this often enough.
They deny the will. They say the will as such does not
exist at all. It is only a mythological creation. Ziehen

expresses himself a little more cautiously of course, but he still arrives at some strange results though he will no doubt take care not to take them to the ultimate conclusion. I would like to read you a few more statements from his last lecture, from which you will see that although he drew the conclusions, he nevertheless still plays around with the nonexistence of the will. For he says, "What about the concept of responsibility?"

He cannot find the will, but in answer to the question about the concept of responsibility he says,

This does indeed contradict physiological psychology. For this told us that our actions are based on absolute necessity, (i.e., in the physical sense) and are the necessary product of our sensations and memory pictures. Thus we can blame a person for a bad deed just as little as we can blame a flower for its ugliness. Therefore an action is still bad—also in a psychological sense—but not directly blameworthy. The terms blame and responsibility, to put it briefly, are a religious or social matter. So we can disregard them here. To recapitulate, psychology does not deny absolute laws of aesthetics and ethics, provided they are seen to be in another sphere, but psychology itself is confined to the empirical realm, to empirical laws only.

This is perfectly natural. If external nature is only *dreamt* about, then we see some people doing one good deed after another and others who keep on attacking people for no reason at all. Just as one flower is beautiful and another ugly according to natural law, one person may be what is called a good person. But on no account should the goodness or hatefulness be explained as meaning more than a flower's beauty or ugliness. So the logical conclusion is,

We can blame a person for a bad deed just as little as we can blame a flower for its ugliness. Therefore an action is still bad—also in a psychological sense—but not directly blameworthy. The terms blame and responsibility, to put it briefly, are a religious or social matter. [Not a matter of understanding but purely a religious or social matter.] So we can disregard them here. To recapitulate, psychology does not deny absolute laws of aesthetics and ethics, provided they are seen to be in another sphere, but psychology is confined to the empirical realm, to empirical laws only.

Ziehen continues to express himself cautiously, and does not yet create a world view. For if one does form a view of life from this, there is no longer any possibility of holding a person responsible for his actions if one takes the stand of the author of this book, this lecture. This is what comes of people dreaming about the outer world. They would wake up the moment they accept what spiritual science says about the outer world. But just think, these people have a science that makes them actually admit that they know nothing at all about what points the way from the external body to the human *I.* Yet what is bound to be living in the *I?* First of all the laws of aesthetics, second the laws of logic. All these must live in the *I.* Everything that leads to the will must live in the *I.* There is nothing in this science that can in any way live as a real impulse in the will. There is nothing of that sort in this science. Therefore something else is necessary.

If this science were the only one the world had today, you can imagine people saying, "There are ugly flowers and there are beautiful flowers and nature necessarily makes them so. There are people who murder others, and there are people who do good to others, and they also are like that by nature." Obviously, everything appealing to the will would have to be discarded. So why is it not discarded? You see, if we no longer take the *I* into account, and if we do not accept it as part of what we can know through observation of our world, we must find it in some other way. If we do not want to continue to uphold "social or religious laws," as Ziehen does, we must somehow get people to accept them in another way. That is to say, if we dream with regard to the outer world and with regard to what we see, then what we will has to be stimulated in some other way.

And this way can only be the opposite of dreaming, namely, ecstasy. What lives in the will must enter into it in such a way that the person under no circumstances stops to think about it or realize fully that it is an impulse of will. That is to say, what has to be aimed for in an age like this is that a person does not attempt to have a clear view of the will impulses he accepts, but they should work in him—and this is a fitting image—like wine does when a person is drunk. An impulse that is not brought to full consciousness works in the same way as intoxicating drink does when it robs a person of the full possession of his wits. That is to say, we live in an age when one has to renounce a really close examination of will impulses. Religious denominations would like to provide impulses, but these must not be examined at any price. On no account ought the motivating ideas be submitted to objective scrutiny. It should all enter into the human being by means of ecstasy.

We can actually prove this all over again in the present time. Just try with an open mind to really listen to the way religious impulses are spoken of nowadays. People feel most comfortable if they are told nothing about why they should accept one or the other impulse,

but are spoken to in such a way that they become enthu-
siastic, fired up, they are given ideas they cannot fully
grasp and that surround them with mystery. And the
most highly acclaimed speakers are the ones who fill
people's souls with fire, fire, and yet more fire, and who
pay least attention to whether everybody has conscious
hold of himself. The dreamers come along and say, "We
examine the Gospels. Even if we go so far as to admit
to the existence of Jesus of Nazareth, we find no evidence at all that there was in fact a supersensible being
dwelling in him." We need only remember how many
dreamers there are who simply deny the existence of
Christ because it cannot be proved on the external
physical plane. On the other hand, there are theologians who cannot prove it either, and who therefore
speak about the Christ in as vague a way as possible,
appealing as much as possible to the feelings, drives,
and instincts.

An example of this kind of thing took place in a
strange way in public very recently. On the one hand,
there were the dreamers—it began with Eduard von
Hartmann in the realm of philosophy, and Drews made
a lot of propaganda out of it—and these dreamers went
so far as to deny the whole message of the testaments
by showing that the Mystery of Golgotha is not a historical occurrence.[5] Certainly, it cannot be proved on
the plane of external history but has to be approached
on the spiritual plane. Now these dreamers had opponents. Read all the literature on this issue and you will
see no sign of any thought, no sign of anything scientific; the whole thing consisted of words one can only
describe as drunken and intoxicating words. No sign of
thorough study! The opponents are appealing the
whole time to what will excite unmotivated instincts.
This is how things stand in our life of soul. On the one

hand, there is dreaming, which is supposed to provide a world view grounded in natural science, and on the other hand, there is intoxication, which people are supposed to acquire from the religious confessions. Dreaming and intoxication are the principal factors controlling mankind today. And just as the only way to stop people from dreaming is to wake them up, the only way to overcome intoxication is to look at our inner impulses in total clarity. This means giving people spiritual science that, far from making the soul drunk, awakens the soul to spiritual impulses. But people are not yet ready to go along with this. I have said before that if we offer the challenge of spiritual science to a hardened monist of the Haeckelian school, one who desires only to prove his monism on the basis of natural science, he falls on his face with a thud, metaphorically speaking, he falls down with a loud thud as a matter of course. That is the obvious thing to happen, for he immediately feels he is in a void and his consciousness is completely bowled over. If you take an ordinary person, someone who wants to base his whole world view on natural science, they mean nothing to him; he cannot understand a thing. If he is honest, he will say, "Here we go again, it makes my head spin." Which means he plops down with a thud.

Concerning intoxication, if someone allows himself to sober up properly, it is a straightforward matter of embarking on a truly ennobled inner religious life. The fact that he can familiarize himself with the impulses coming from spiritual science will enable his belief to deepen into concrete concepts. But if you approach someone who does not want to awaken his soul to the ideals of spiritual science, yet you bring them to him and want him to accept them, that is to say, if you bring spiritual science to someone who is completely under

111

the sway of modern theology, he will sober up, in a strange way, like people who have been drunk and have not quite recovered from the organic aftereffects. He gets a hangover. You can really notice it.

If you observe theologians nowadays—and we can do this especially well in the Dornach area where the theologians take more notice of it—if you observe them in cases where spiritual science is familiar to them but still undigested, and if you listen to them, you will find that all they say is basically a kind of hangover, caused by the fact that they ought to acquire ideas and knowledge about spiritual matters, yet still prefer to be drunk with ecstasy over them and to introduce them into people's mental organization in an entirely unmotivated way. They shrink from becoming sober because they cannot bear the thought that it will not bring them enlightenment but a throbbing headache.

These things must absolutely be seen in their historical necessity. If it can come about that spiritual science brings people at least the rudiments of an understanding of how to regain in a new way the sight of what has been lost, how to motivate the will once again, then humanity will acquire in freedom what nature can no longer give us. You see then that a certain necessity underlies our program. The kind of lecture I gave last Friday and have often given, drawing your attention to the development of thinking on the one hand and the development of will on the other, showed how thinking proceeds until we discover the will in it and come out of ourselves through thinking. It also showed how we find the other spectator on the other side, and demonstrates that through the very fact that we bring thinking to the point where we can emerge out of ourselves, we will have a chance not to fall flat on our faces when we are shouted at and awakened.

112

We fall down only because we cannot understand outer processes and have nothing to hold on to when we are awakened from our dreams. What one has to hold on to, so as not to get into the kind of inwardly inorganic, disordered state we call a hangover, is what one can acquire through developing one's thinking. This comes about when the inner spectator I spoke of can emerge unhindered from our inner being. Thus what should be imparted to humanity above all is intimately connected with the real inner laws of human progress.

Yet if you think about what has been said here today and often before, and bear in mind its implications, you will avoid certain obvious mistakes. Some mistakes, of course, will be extremely difficult to avoid, and I will point out just one of these today. Again and again individuals among us say, "There are, for instance, the followers of this or that confession," assuming in this case that we live among a more or less Catholic population "who have their Catholic priest." Our friends very often believe that if they explain to this priest that we do represent Christianity, speak about the Mystery of Golgotha in the right way, and do not deny the existence of Christ, we will be able to gain the priest's friendship.

This way of thinking is completely wrong. You will never win these people over by showing them that we do not deny what they are duty bound to preach. We simply cannot do that. Actually you would get on better with these people if you were in a position to say that you are people who do not believe in Christ. Then they would say, "You see, there are people who do not believe in Christ. They do not belong to us. We shall stick to our community who are content to learn from us about Christ through ecstasy." They do not say that,

but that is how they act. Yet when other people besides *them* affirm the existence of Christ and even maintain they have positive knowledge of Christ, and we become the sort of people who follow our own way, and who want to present Christ in a different way from them: they then become far worse enemies than they would be if our friends were to deny the existence of Christ. For they consider it *their* privilege to present Christianity, and our mistake is precisely to present it in another way.

Therefore you only make certain theologians furious with spiritual science if you tell them, "We speak of the Christ." You would make them far less angry if you were able to say—which of course you are not—"We deny the existence of Christ." What infuriates them is that we refer to Christ in a different context. Out of the best intentions in the world our friends will very easily say, "What do you want? We are on a completely Christian footing." That is the worst thing you can possibly say to them, for that is just what goes so much against the grain with them.

This touches again on an area where we encounter freedom and necessity in a very special way. The main thing I keep trying to bring home to people is that we should not take these ideas lightly. Freedom and necessity are among the most important human concepts, and you have to realize time and again that we have to gather a great number of ideas to arrive at a more or less correct understanding of the concepts of freedom and necessity.

Where would it lead if present-day humanity were to follow nothing but natural necessity? People would obviously dream more and more, until they had nothing left but a dreary grey in grey, and they would become less and less able to use their will, until they

114

reached actual paralysis of the will. That is necessity. Out of the freedom of spiritual science people must obviously work to counteract this; for the time is now dawning when we will have to acquire our essential freedom out of an inner necessity which we ourselves acknowledge. Of course we might all say, "We are not going to concern ourselves with what is supposed to happen." In that case things would come about as described. Yet that things can be different is a necessity, a necessity, however, that can only be taken hold of through understanding. We might call it a free necessity, a genuine and absolute necessity.

Here again the concepts freedom and necessity come very close together. It might sometimes have seemed as though I was only playing with the words "dreaming and intoxication." That was most certainly not the case. You can find individual examples, and I could tell you many, many more, of the way people speak, as though in a kind of dream, about outer reality. For instance, a particular objection is often raised against what I say in anthroposophical lectures. A pet remark is, "But how can you prove that?" meaning that people require to have what is presented to them proved by comparing it with outer reality. They assume that an idea is valid only if one can point to its physical counterpart, and that this external counterpart is the proof. This is such an extremely obvious idea, that people think they are great logicians if they say, "You see, it all depends on being able to prove that a concept links up with its counterpart in outer reality."

You can easily point out that this is no great logic but proper dream logic. When people say things like this, I usually give the answer that even where the external sense world is concerned you cannot prove reality, for if someone had never in his life seen a whale, you could

115

never prove the existence of whales through logic alone, could you? Pointing to the reality is something quite different from proving a thing. So much for dream-logic.

I can put it even more plainly. Suppose I paint a portrait of a living person, and someone gives as his objective opinion "This portrait is very like the person," and goes on to explain that this is so because when he compares the portrait with the person, they both look the same. The likeness is due to the fact that the portrait agrees with reality. Does the correspondence to external reality cause the likeness? Why does he say the picture is like the model? Because it corresponds to external reality. The external reality is what is true. Now imagine that the model dies, and we look at his portrait thirty years later. Is it no longer like him, thirty years later, because it does not agree with external reality any more? The person is no longer there. We can assume that he was cremated a long time ago. Does the likeness depend on the external reality being there? Clear thinking knows it does not. In the case of dream-thinking one can say that in order to prove anything one has to be able to point to external reality. But this is only true for dream-thinking, dream-logic. For surely, just because a person passes from existence to nonexistence, a portrait of him does not change from being like him to being unlike him!

You see, many things can be made into a necessity if people want to adapt their logic accordingly, especially when we find in every article about logic nowadays "The truth of a concept consists in, or can be proved by, the fact that one can point to the external reality in the physical world." But this definition of truth is nonsense, and this becomes evident in cases like the comparison with the portrait. If you consult so-called scientific books today—not the kind that deal with pure science—all they do is give descriptions, and if we stick to descriptions, what does it matter if we remain in mere dreams? If some people want to describe nothing more than the dream of outer life and do not pretend to build a world view, let them. However, a world view based on this is a dream view. And we can see that. Wherever this step is taken, you usually find dream-philosophy.

It is quite ridiculous how unable people are to think, that is to say, to think in such a way that their thinking is based on the element on which it ought to be based. I have copied out a statement Professor Ziehen makes on page 208 of these lectures, in which he wants particularly to point out that we cannot find the will that underlies an action. He puts it like this, "Thinking consists of a series of mental images, and the psychic part"—that is, the soul content—"of an action is also a series of mental images with the particular characteristic that the last link in the chain is a mental image of movement."

There is the clock. The will is eliminated, isn't it? I see the clock. That is now a mental image. The will does not exist and I see the clock. This clock has an effect on me in some way by setting my cerebral cortex into some sort of motion, and then passes from the cerebral cortex into a kind of motor zone, as physiology tells us. One thing passes on to the next. This is the thought image of movement. I have first of all an image of the clock, and the image of the movement succeeds the activity of the imagining the movement, not by way of will but by way of the image of movement. "I have only a series of mental images," says Ziehen. Thinking consists of a series of mental images, and the psychic part of an action is also a series of mental images. The will is unquestionably eliminated. It is not there. First of all I observe the clock and then the movement of my hand. That is all.

You can track down the logic this contains by translating this statement into another one. You can just as well say, "Thinking consists of a series of mental images. So far so good. And when we look at a machine, the psychic process is just another mental image, with the particular characteristic that the last link in the chain is a mental image of a moving machine." One is exactly the same as the other. You have merely eliminated the machine's driving power. You have merely added the mental image of the moving machine to what you were thinking before.

This is what this dream-logic consists of. Where the outer world is concerned, a person who applies dream-logic does of course admit the existence of impulses of some sort, but not in the case of the inner world, because he wants to eliminate the will. Ziehen's whole book is full of dream-logic of this kind, eliminating the will. At the same time of course the *I* is also being eliminated, which is interesting. According to him, the *I* is also nothing more than a series of mental images. He actually explicitly says so.

The following interesting thing can happen. Forgive me if I let you into some of the intimate secrets involved in the preparation of a lecture like today's. I had to give today's lecture, didn't I? I wanted to bring you not just an overall picture of what I had to say but also some details. So I had to get this book out and look at it again, which I did. I could of course not read you the whole book but had to limit myself to a selection of passages. I certainly wanted to show you that today's world view based on dream-science cannot include the will, the will is really not there. I have shown you what the author has to say about it in this book of his. I wanted to draw

118

your special attention to what the author says about the will, that is to say, what he says against it. So I look up "will" at the back of the book; aha, page 205 and following, and turn there to see what he says about it. I did tell you today too, though, that in the first instance the will is only perceptible in the physical world in the *I*. So when we speak of the true *I*, we actually have to speak of the *I* that wills. Therefore I also had to show you how the person who has nothing but a dream view based on science speaks of the *I*. To show you that he simply denies the will, I read you the passage from "Mental image of movement" to "the will is eliminated."

I also wanted to read you something briefly on what he says about the *I*. So I turned to the index again—but *I* does not occur at all! That is entirely consistent, of course. So we have as a matter of course a book on physiological psychology or psychiatry that does not mention the *I!* There is no reference to it in the index and, if you go through it, you will see that only the mental image of the *I* occurs, just a mental image of course. The author lets mental images pass, for they are only another word for mechanical processes of the brain. But the *I* as such does not figure at all; it is eliminated.

You see it has already become an ideal, this eliminating of the *I*. But if humanity follows nature, then by the sixth post-Atlantean epoch the *I* will be eliminated altogether in earnest, for if the impulses of will proceeding from the center of one's being are lacking, people will hardly speak of an *I*. During the fifth epoch human beings have had the task to advance to taking up an *I*. But they could lose this *I* again if they do not really search for it through inner effort. Those who know anything at all about this aspect of the world could tell you things about the number of people one already meets who say they sense a weakness of their *I*. How many people are there today who do not know what to do with themselves, because they do not know how to fill their souls with spiritual content? Here we are facing a chapter of unspeakable misery of soul that is more widespread in our time than one usually imagines. For the number of people unable to cope with life because they cannot find impulses within themselves to support their *I* in the world of appearances is constantly growing.

This in turn is connected with something I have often spoken about here, namely, that up to now it was essential that people should work towards acquiring a conception of their *I*. And we live in the time when this is finally being properly acquired. You know that in Latin, which was the language of the fourth epoch, the word *ego* was only used as an exception. People then did not speak of the *I*, it was still contained in the verb. The more world evolution, and language too, approached the fifth post-Atlantean epoch, the more the *I* became separated. The Christ impulse is to help us find this *I* in the right way. The fact that in Central Europe in particular this *I* is uniting itself in its purest form with the Christ impulse is expressed in the language itself, in that through the inner necessity of evolution the word for *I* (German: *Ich*) is built up out of the initials of Christ: I - C - H, Jesus Christ.

This may well seem a dream to those who want to stay nowadays in the realm of dream-science. Those who wake themselves from this dream view of life will appreciate the great and significant truth of this fact. The *I* expresses the connection the human being has to Christ. But people have to cherish it by filling it with the content of spiritual science. However, they will be able to do this only if with the help of science they make freedom a necessity. Really, how could people have said in earlier times that it used to be the normal thing for people to remember previous incarnations? Yet for our coming earth lives it will be normal.

Just as in the fifth post-Atlantean epoch human beings have to take hold of their *I* and bring it to life, so it will be the normal thing in the future for people to have a stronger and stronger memory of their previous lives. We could just as well say, "Spiritual science is the right preparation for remembering earlier lives in the right way." But those who run away from spiritual science will not be able to bring this memory of past lives up into consciousness. Their inner being will feel something lacking.

That is to say, people will fall into two categories. One group will know that when they examine their innermost soul, it will lead them back into earlier lives. The others will feel an inner urge that comes to expression as a longing. Something does not want to emerge. Throughout their whole incarnation something will not want to come up, but will remain unknown like a thought one searches and cannot find. This will be due to insufficient preparation for remembering previous earth lives.

When we speak of these things, we are speaking of something real, absolutely real. You have to have properly taken hold of the *I* through spiritual science if you are to remember it in later earth lives. Is there anything you can remember without making a mental picture of it? Need we wonder that people cannot yet remember the *I* when they did not have a mental picture of it in earlier epochs? Everything is understandable with true

121

logic. But the dream-logic of the so-called monism of our time is obviously always going to oppose what has to come into being through the true logic of spiritual science.

NOTES

Lecture I

[1]Immanuel Kant, 1724–1804, German philosopher of the Enlightenment. For his antinomian chart see his book *Critique of Pure Reason* published in 1781.

[2]Matthias Claudius, 1740–1815, German poet.

[3]K. F. E. Thrandorff, 1782–1863. Wrote an open letter entitled "The Devil—No Dogmatic Bogy" to a preacher in Berlin in 1853.

[4]Ernst Haeckel, 1834–1919, German scientist and philosopher. Adherent of Monism.

Lecture II

[1]Johann Wolfgang von Goethe, 1749–1832, German poet, playwright, and novelist.

[2]Karl August, Duke of Weimar, 1757–1828, Duke of Saxony and Weimar 1758-1828.

[3]*Faust*, dramatic poem by Johann Wolfgang von Goethe.

[4]Madame de Staël (Germaine de Staël), 1766–1817, French writer and intellectual.

[5]Franz von Spaun, 1753–1826, German essayist. The quotation from *Faust* is from Part I, "Night," Translated by Sir Theodore Martin. Everyman's Library, (London: Dent, 1971).

[6]Max Reinhardt, 1873–1943, director of the German theater in Berlin.

[7]Rudolf Steiner, *An Outline of Occult Science*, (Spring Valley, N.Y.: Anthroposophic Press, 1972).

Lecture III

[1]See lectures of December 3 and December 10, 1915, in Berlin in *Aus dem mitteleuropäischen Geistesleben* (Of Central

European Cultural and Spiritual Life), GA 65. Not yet translated.

Lecture IV

[1]Baruch Spinoza, 1632–1677, Dutch pantheist philosopher. The example of a stone being pushed into motion can be found in his sixty-second letter of 1674.
[2]Rudolf Steiner, *Philosophy of Spiritual Activity*, (Hudson, N.Y.: Anthroposophic Press, 1986).
[3]Gotthold Ephraim Lessing, 1729–1781, German poet, playwright, and critic.
[4]*Nibelungenlied*, a Middle High German epic of about 1200, telling of the life of Siegfried, his marriage to Kriemhild, his wooing of Brunhild on behalf of Gunther, his murder by Hagen, and the revenge of Kriemhild.
[5]Parsifal, a hero of mythology and various epics and romances, especially the one by Wolfram von Eschenbach.

Lecture V

[1]Arthur Schopenhauer, 1788–1860, German philosopher.
[2]Rudolf Steiner, *Knowledge of the Higher Worlds and Its Attainment*, (Hudson, N.Y.: Anthroposophic Press, 1986).
[3]Bernhard Bolzano, 1781–1848, mathematician and logician from Bohemia.
[4]Theodor Ziehen, 1862–1950. Published *Theory of Knowledge on the basis of Psycho-Physiology and Physics* in 1913.
[5]Eduard von Hartmann, 1842–1906, German philosopher. Arthur Drews, 1865–1935, philosopher. Denied the existence of Jesus.

FOR FURTHER READING

Rudolf Steiner intended these carefully written volumes to serve as a foundation to all of the later, more advanced anthroposophical writings and lecture courses.

THE PHILOSOPHY OF SPIRITUAL ACTIVITY by Rudolf Steiner. "Is human action free?" asks Steiner in his most important philosophical work. By first addressing the nature of knowledge, Steiner cuts across the ancient debate of real or illusory human freedom. A painstaking examination of human experience as a polarity of percepts and concepts shows that only in thinking does one escape the compulsion of natural law. Steiner's argument arrives at the recognition of the self-sustaining, universal reality of thinking that embraces both subjective and objective validity. Free acts can be performed out of love for a "moral intuition" grasped ever anew by a living thinking activity. Steiner scrutinizes numerous world-views and philosophical positions and finally indicates the relevance of his conclusion to human relations and life's ultimate questions. (262 pp)   Paper, $8.95 #1074; Cloth, $18.00 #1073

KNOWLEDGE OF THE HIGHER WORLDS AND ITS ATTAINMENT by Rudolf Steiner. Rudolf Steiner's fundamental work on the path to higher knowledge explains in detail the exercises and disciplines a student must pursue in order to attain a wakeful experience of supersensible realities. The stages of Preparation, Enlightenment, and Initiation are described, as is the transformation of dream-life and the meeting with the Guardian of the Threshold. Moral exercises for developing each of the spiritual lotus petal organs ("chakras") are given in accordance with the rule of taking three steps in moral development for each step into spiritual knowledge. The path described here is a safe one which will not interfere with the student's ability to lead a normal outer life. (272 pp)   Paper, $6.95 #80; Cloth, $14.00 #363

THEOSOPHY, AN INTRODUCTION TO THE SUPERSENSIBLE KNOWLEDGE OF THE WORLD AND THE DESTINATION OF MAN by Rudolf Steiner. In this work Steiner carefully explains many of the basic concepts and terminologies of anthroposophy. The book begins with a sensitive description of the primordial trichotomy: body, soul, and spirit, elaborating the various higher members of the human constitution. A discussion of reincarnation and karma follows. The next and longest chapter presents, in a vast panorama, the seven regions of the soul world, the seven regions of the land of spirits, and the soul's journey after death through these worlds. A brief discussion of the path to higher knowledge follows. (195 pp)   Paper, $6.95 #155; Cloth, $9.95 #154

AN OUTLINE OF OCCULT SCIENCE by Rudolf Steiner. This work begins with a thorough discussion and definition of the term "occult" science. A description of the supersensible nature of the human being follows, along with a discussion of dreams, sleep, death, life between death and rebirth, and reincarnation. In the fourth chapter evolution is described from the perspective of initiation science. The fifth chapter characterizes the training a student must undertake as a preparation for initiation. The sixth and seventh chapters consider the future evolution of the world and more detailed observations regarding supersensible realities. (388 pp)   Paper, $9.95 #113, Cloth, $16.00 #112

To order send a check including $2 for postage and handling (NY State residence please add local sales tax) to Anthroposophic Press, Bells Pond, Star Route, Hudson, NY 12534. Credit Card phone orders are accepted (518) 851-2054. (Prices subject to change)

A catalogue of over 300 titles is free on request.